MATTHEWS. H.
CHARACTER & SYMBOL IN
SHAKESPEARE'S PLAYS   822S

CHARACTER AND SYMBOL IN
SHAKESPEARE'S PLAYS

CHARACTER & SYMBOL
IN
SHAKESPEARE'S
PLAYS

A STUDY OF CERTAIN CHRISTIAN AND
PRE-CHRISTIAN ELEMENTS IN THEIR
STRUCTURE AND IMAGERY

BY

HONOR MATTHEWS

1969

CHATTO & WINDUS
LONDON

Published by
Chatto & Windus Ltd
40 William IV Street
London, W.C.2

*

Clarke, Irwin and Co. Ltd
Toronto

*First published 1962 by the Cambridge University Press
Reprinted 1969 by Chatto & Windus*

SBN 7011 1422 3

Printed in Great Britain by
William Lewis (Printers) Ltd
Cardiff

PREFACE

I should like to recognise the help of the many students of Goldsmiths' College who have singlemindedly striven with me to learn of the plays' significance through recreating them on the stage and submitting these interpretations to the acid test of practical production.

H.M.

CONTENTS

CONTENTS

PART III

'A LASTING SPRING'

INTRODUCTION

The purpose of this book is to offer to the reader a thread which may lead him to a finer appreciation of one pattern discernible in the complexity of Shakespeare's created world. It is the pattern formed by the concepts of sin, judgment and redemption. Throughout the plays there ring, for all who care to listen, echoes from the culture which was their author's inheritance, and the importance of these echoes must inevitably be differently assessed by readers for whom their sound is clear or faint. It is the belief of the writer that some very simple and even obvious reminders of the sources of such resonances will attune the reader's ear to a music which is a significant part of the plays' content, and such reminders therefore precede the consideration of the selected themes in Shakespeare's own work. If this study helps any lover of the plays to be more vitally aware of the stuff of which such masterpieces are actually made and therefore to enjoy them more acutely, the writer's purpose will have been achieved.

The threefold pattern to which the reader's attention is invited is, of course, clearly laid down in the teaching of the Christian Church and formed the raw material of a powerful drama on the medieval stage. Miracle and morality plays were acted until the last decade of the sixteenth century, and Elizabethan audiences were the direct inheritors of a drama which reflected the principal ideas and values of a unified view of life. Basic elements in their outlook were their conception of man's place in a divinely created universe and of his ability to know and to choose between good and evil. Hence came the belief in the reality of sin bringing with it the fear of God's justice, the desire for his mercy and the realisation of a clash between them. The primary sin, committed first by Lucifer, was conceived as ambition—the desire to be as God, and this sin was reflected in all men's lesser attempts to transcend the proper limits imposed on them by their Creator. The only excuses which could be pleaded in mitigation of man's admitted failure were the

I

strength of his temptation by forces of evil outside himself and the frailty of his own nature which made him a ready prey to deception. No excuses, however, could alter facts, and man remained lost unless he received the help of a Saviour who could ensure the mystic reconciliation of justice with mercy.

The stories embodying these concepts are the prototypes after which much of Shakespeare's greatest work is shaped. Up to the writing of *Measure for Measure* there is observable a passionate interest in what an Elizabethan homilist called 'the Luciferian sin' and an almost obsessional concern with the irreconcilability of justice and mercy. Already, however, a counter-subject is discernible accompanying these themes, one which also had its place in the medieval drama. The horror of man's predicament is that, while it is essential for him to perceive the good that he may choose it, he is constantly misled by his inability to penetrate below the false appearances with which the evil powers in the universe attempt to destroy him. This cause of his continual need of mercy, not judgment, from his God and his fellow-men gradually assumes a place in the plays so important that it replaces Shakespeare's earlier concern with the simple opposition of justice and mercy. Finally, there is the third part of the triptych to be considered: the hope of redemption, a new life in a new world. Here the Christian archetype is the return of the suffering Saviour in glory at the end of the present age to bring the final judgment of eternal life or eternal death. This element is present in Shakespeare's earliest dramatic conceptions, but it becomes dominant only in his last phase, and here the sources of the imagery change. No longer does the Christian symbolism stand alone, although it never disappears. What does disappear completely, however, is the finality of Doomsday and the cataclysm of damnation.

In reminding the reader of some of the traditional material which seems to have been present in Shakespeare's mind as he worked, narrow and arbitrary limits must be set. No attempt can be made here to summarise the content of medieval philosophy or theology, nor would such material be relevant to our present purpose. Only such elements of this thought as were lively in the minds of the dramatist or his audience and were, therefore, taken for granted by them in interpreting their experience and in assessing its values are of importance. Because we are concerned with the making of plays, the illustrations used will be sought principally in the popular medieval and sixteenth-century drama, for it is not without interest to remember what audiences and dramatists alike had been conditioned to accept as the normal stuff of theatrical entertainment. Such entertainment was frequently religious in its overt content, but it had never been confined to the Christian drama which is still familiar because so many examples have survived in written form. Countless dramatic and semi-dramatic activities going back to pre-Christian times survived in Elizabethan England and played some part in informing Shakespeare's imagination. It is, of course, difficult to know with any reassuring certainty the significance in Shakespeare's picture of life of these echoes and recurrences. Some may be the merest stock-in-trade of his surface mind, standing out to us only because they are no longer the stock-in-trade of our own. When, however, he makes them the media of outstandingly fine imagery—condensed, musical, ambiguous—or uses them in moments of intense dramatic emotion, when his powers are obviously fully extended and his involvement with his material deep and effective, then we can assume that the images and associations are significant and must not be discounted.

PART I

THE LUCIFERIAN SIN: REBELLION

CHAPTER I

THE ATTACK ON THE THRONE

1. SOME PRE-SHAKESPEAREAN STATEMENTS

Each of the four cycles of miracle plays that have come down to us in some measure of completeness opens with the presentation of the first sin. This is, of course, the original rebellion of Lucifer, and in each cycle it receives all the emphasis of which a well-developed dramatic tradition is capable. Raised on pageant or mansion stage is seated God the Father, and round him stand the angelic hierarchies.

> Lord, throughe thy grace and mighte thou hast us wrought:
> Nyne orders of Angelles here as you may see: . . .
> In thie bliss full righte they be,
> And I the principall lord here in thie sight.
>
> Chester Plays: *Fall of Lucifer*, ll. 28 ff.[1]

When Lucifer falls from his high eminence he makes a visible descent, and his white and golden garments are changed for the black or shaggy tights and horrific mask made familiar by countless carvings and paintings.

In the *Ludus Coventriae*[2] the proclamation, which serves as programme to what follows, introduces Man's principal antagonist thus:

> But Lucifer that angel so gay
> In such pomp then is he pite
> And set in so great pride
> That God's seat he ginneth to take
> His Lord's peer himself to make.
>
> *Proclamation*, ll. 18 ff.

[1] Early English Text Society: Extra Series, LXII.
[2] *Ibid.*, Extra Series, CXX. Spelling and punctuation modernised by the author.

7

After his fall Lucifer tempts Eve as he had done the angels:

> Of this apple if thou wilt bite
> Even as God is so shall ye be.
> Wise of cunning as I you plight
> Like unto God in all degree.
> Sun and moon and stars bright
> Fish and fowl both sound and sea
> At your bidding both day and night
> All things shall be in your power.
> Ye shall be God's peer.   *Fall of Man*, ll. 182 ff.

Adam replies by asserting the penalty of an unlawful claim to equality:

> I dare not touch thy hand for dread . . .
> If that we do this sinful deed
> We shall be dead by God's judgment.   ll. 221–6

The nature of the fault is continually re-emphasised by the symbol of *the throne*, deserved or usurped as the case may be:

> *Lucifer*: A worthier lord forsooth am I
> And worthier than He ever will I be.
> In evidence that I am more worthy
> I will go sit in God's seat
> Above sun and moon and stars in sky
> I am now set as ye may see,
> Now worship me for most mighty . . .
> Sitting in my seat.   *Fall of Lucifer*, ll. 53 ff.

The symbolism is developed in more detail in the Chester cycle:

> *God*: And here I sett you next my Chayre,
> My love to you is so fervent,
> Looke ye fall not in no dispayre,
> touche not my throne by non assent.   ll. 67 ff.

When God has withdrawn, Lucifer approaches the throne:

> *Lucifer*: I am pereles and prince of pryde,
> for God himself shynes not so sheene.
> Here will I sit now in this stid . . .

> All Angelles turn to me, I redd,
> And to your soveraigne knele on your knee!...
> *Lightburne*: And I ame next of the same degree...
> Methink if I might sit by the
> all heaven shold do me reverence...
> *Lucifer*: thoughe God come here, I will not hence,
> but sit right here before his face.   ll. 163 ff.

The throne may easily become the sign of the tyrant who usurps or misuses the power delegated by God and thus reflects the sin of Lucifer. In the Chester *Slaying of the Innocents*, for example, the Messenger addresses Herod:

> Haile! comly kyng, sitting in see.   l. 73

The clearest type of the usurper in later stages of the Christian story is Antichrist, and he is given an interesting play in the Chester cycle. To convince all beholders that he is really Christ he first raises two men from the dead and then undertakes to raise himself, after he has died and been buried.

> *Antichrist*: I Ryse! now Reverence dose to me....
> *Primus Rex*: A! lorde, welcome must thou be!
> that thou art god now leeve we;
> therfore goe, sitt up in thy See,
> And keep our Sacrifice.
> *Secundus Rex*: for sooth in Seat thou shalt be sett
> and honoured with lambe and Geatt!
> *Tertius Rex*: O! Gracious lord, goe, sitt down then!
> And we shall, knelinge on our knen,
> Worship thee as thyne owne men.
> *Coming of Antichrist*, ll. 164 ff.

As Antichrist mounts his throne, a later voice may fall faintly on the ear:

> Cousin of Buckingham!...
> Give me thy hand. Thus high by thy advice
> And thy assistance, is King Richard seated:
> *Richard III*, IV, ii, 1-5

When the true Christ returns crowned to make the final judgment, he says to his apostles:

> Come forth I shall sit you between
> And all fulfil that I have plight.[1]   *Doomsday*

These accumulated associations of the throne both with the true God and with his false images give an added irony to the scene thus described in the Condemnation and Scourging of the *Ludus Coventriae*.

And when he is scourged they put upon him a cloth of silk, and setting him on a stool, and putting a crown of thorns on his head, with forks, and the Jews kneeling to Christ and taking him a sceptre and scorning him.

Such usage gradually built up the complex of associations which led to the repeated use on the later stage of that 'creaking throne', mocked by Ben Jonson when it 'comes down the boys to please',[2] but so significant to Hamlet when he watched Claudius smiling and drinking upon it, or to Macbeth as he sits, wishing only 'to be safely thus'. Menenius, in emphasising the absolute power of Coriolanus, declares:

> He sits in his State, as a thing made for Alexander.... He wants nothing of a God but Eternity and a Heaven to throne in.   v, iv, 22–6

The king on his throne is the most vivid symbol of degree possible in simple theatrical terms, and this in itself is a valid reason for the preference for a kingly hero shown by all those dramatists, Greek as well as Christian, who write of the act of *hubris* in a hierarchical society. Nevertheless, the concept had often to be dealt with in other terms, as for example those of the relationships between man and woman, or parents and children. When Gloucester taunts Queen Margaret with the jibe that she:

> might still have worn the petticoat,
> And ne'er have stol'n the breech from Lancaster,
>
> *3 Henry VI*, v, v, 23–4

the medieval dramatist had already declared in the *Ludus Coventriae*:

> Woman, thou soughtest his sinning
> And bade him break my bidding

---

[1] *York Mystery Plays*, ed. by J. S. Purvis, D.D.
[2] *Every Man in his Humour*, Prologue, l. 16.

Therefore thou shalt be underling
To man's bidding bend.

Fall of Man, ll. 333 ff.

Goneril and Regan, calmly discussing their father's follies, are like-wise the direct descendants of a medieval prototype, that of Cain who denies to Adam the respect which Abel gladly pays:

> *Cain*: As to my father let us now tee
> To know what shall be his talking,
> And that I hold it but vanity
> To go to him for any speaking
> To lere of his law.
> For if I have good anow plenty
> I can be merry, so might thee;
> Though my father I never see
> I give not there of an hawe.
> *Abel*: Right sovereign father, seemly, sad and sure
> Ever we thank you in heart, body and thought
> And always shall while our lives may endure.

Cain and Abel, ll. 14 ff.

The morality plays develop the notion of man's proper 'degree' in the cosmos. In *Nature*,[1] for example, Mankind is taught to recog-nise his own rung on the ladder between the angels and the beasts. He has received divine gifts of understanding and 'free election'.

> And in this point am I half angelic
> Unto thy heavenly spirits almost egal.

Reason, however, instructs him in the ease with which he may lose his privileged position once he deserts reason for sensuality:

> So that there is no difference in that at the least
> Betwixt man and an unreasonable beast.

The voice might be that of Friar Lawrence as he blames Romeo for indulging in 'the unreasonable fury of a beast'.

With the steady secularisation of the drama during the sixteenth century the Christian material that has been considered so far no longer received direct dramatic expression. It was, however,

---

[1] *Early English Dramatists*, ed. by J. S. Farmer (1907).

widely presented in a form that people apparently found only less entertaining than the drama, that is the sermon. The continuity of direct transmission must be briefly illustrated if the force of the old prototypes in the Elizabethan mind is to be fairly assessed.

The primal sin remains rebellion, and the arch-rebels are still Lucifer and Adam, who maintained their central place in men's imaginations until long after *Paradise Lost* was written. Such concepts can be watched on their gradual progress from medieval to Renaissance forms. In the writings of Erasmus, for example, they are still stated in the old religious terminology:

Among the manifold evils which draw mankind to everlasting damnation there be two chief and principal mischiefs: . . . too much trust in one's own self and despair. The one cometh of a presumptuous mind against God . . . the other . . . by considering the righteous judgment of God without remembrance of his mercy. . . . Is it not a point of great wickedness not to knowledge thy Maker? . . . Unhappy Lucifer was bold to do this first which . . . said in his heart: 'I will get up above in heaven . . . I will climb up above the height of the clouds: I will be like to Almighty God.' . . . Truly, if God spared not proud presumptuous angels, but cast them headlong down, . . . what deserveth man?[1]

It is, however, in the swing from a predominantly religious to a predominantly social emphasis that the change from medieval to Elizabethan pre-dispositions of mind is most clearly revealed. Not of course that the two spheres were then disassociated, for crime against the state remained sin against God. By the Homily '*Against Disobedience and Wilful Rebellion*' (1562)[2] man is taught that order

is the very root of all virtues and the cause of all felicity . . . with the breach of obedience and breaking in of rebellion all vices and miseries did break in and overwhelm the world . . . the first author of which rebellion was Lucifer, the grand captain and father of rebels . . . the brightest and most glorious of the angels. . . . Thus do you see that neither heaven nor paradise could suffer any rebellion in them. . . . Thus

---

[1] *De Immensa* 1523. Translated as *A Sermon of the Exceeding Mercy of God*, confiscated on first appearance but reissued 1533 and 1547.

[2] *Certaine sermons or homilies appointed to be read in churches in the time of the late Queen Elizabeth*. . . Reprinted 1623.

became rebellion . . . both the first and the greatest and the very root of all other sins.

But although the root was recognised to be rebellion against God, it was the fruit, rebellion against the state, with which the Elizabethan mind was particularly concerned. Sir John Cheke's *The Hurt of Sedition*, addressed to the rebels in Norfolk in 1549, will serve as a typical statement from among thousands.

He that faulteth, faulteth against God's ordinance who hath forbidden all faults, and therefore ought again to be punished by God's ordinance who is the Reformer of faults. For He saith: Leave the punishment to Me and I will revenge thee. But the magistrate is the ordinance of God appointed by Him with the sword of punishment.

All the medieval horror at man's rebellion against God was transferred to the very thought of his rebellion against the king, and the cumulative pressure of disapproval of any form of rebellion in Tudor England is hard to imagine adequately. Here is the voice of Tyndale, whose *Obedience of a Christian Man* went through eight editions before 1561:

There is no power but of God. Whoever therefore resisteth the power, resisteth the ordinance of God. They that resist shall receive to themselves damnation.

In the Homily on disobedience already quoted we read:

All sinnes possible to be committed against God or man be contained in rebellion: which sinnes if a man list to name by the accustomed names of the seven capital or deadly sins as Pride, Envy, Wrath, Covetousnesse, Sloth, Gluttonie and Lecherie, he shall find them all in rebellion and amongst rebels. . . . First ambition and desire to be aloft . . . *a Luciferian pride.* . . .[1]

No excuse is given to the Lightbournes, Tyrrels and First and Second Murderers of the coming plays, for the subject is instructed not to obey the ruler who commands anything contrary to the ordinances of God. Even so, however, he 'must not withstand violently or rebel against rulers or make any insurrection, sedition

---

[1] Italics the author's.

or tumults either by force of arms or otherwise', but 'must in such case suffer patiently'. One reason given for this is the difficulty—pointed out in *Richard II* by the Bishop of Carlisle—of finding anyone fitted to judge a king.[1] The bad man will be seeking his own ends if he does so, and the good will accept a bad prince as God's own punishment for the sins of the people. In view of this chorus of condemnation, Shakespeare's treatment of the rebels in *Henry IV* becomes remarkable.[2]

Shakespeare accepted the myth of Lucifer's rebellion as the archetype of sin and, like his contemporaries, found an acceptable reflection of it in the recent history of his own country. The Elizabethans were taught by both homilists and historians to view the fate of Richard III as a supreme example of rebellion and its aftermath. With the exception of the anonymous author of *The True Tragedie of Richard III*, however, their dramatists found their symbols—and with good reason—in more remote and less politically explosive material. Among them Shakespeare alone traced in English history a picture of sin, justice and redemption such as his fathers had found in the Bible stories, and the Greeks in the legends of Agamemnon and Oedipus.

In *The True Tragedie of Richard III* (1594),[3] however, the Luciferian hero's despair and death are related to his own wrongdoing with both psychological and literary skill:

> *Richard*: The goale is got, and golden Crowne is wonne
> And well deservest thou to weare the same,
> That ventured hast thy bodie and thy soule.
> But what bootes Richard now the diademe
> of kingdome got, by murther of his friends,
> My fearfull shadow that still follows me
> Hath sommond me before the severe judge. . . .
>
> Nay what canst thou do to purge thee of thy guilt?
> Even repent, crave mercie for thy damned fact,
> Appeale for mercy to thy righteous God,

---

[1] See IV, i, 121—'What subject can give sentence on a king?'

[2] It might be compared with the sympathy he evinced for a Jew and a Moor, also members of unpopular minorities in Elizabethan London.

[3] Malone Society Reprint, 1929.

14

Ha, repent, not I, crave mercy they that list.
My God is none of mine. . . .   ll. 1398–1420

His remorse culminates in genuine hysteria before Bosworth:

Richard: The headless peeres comes preasing for revenge . . .
How came the foe in, preasing so near?
Where, where slept the garrison that should a kept them back?
ll. 1884–1909

The *True Tragedie* brings us to the time when Shakespeare was beginning his own history plays and to them we can now turn.[1]

2. THE BREACH OF DEGREE

Henry VI; *Richard III*

The three parts of *Henry VI* together with their conclusion, *Richard III*, reveal both Shakespeare's use of the traditional attitudes and material and also the personal idiosyncrasies which develop continuously through his work. In this tetralogy he is concerned with justice and finally with salvation, or mercy. Man's sin, however, is stated not in the terms of the archetypal rebellion of Lucifer, but of its derivative, the more general breach of degree; and the salvation, when it comes, is presented in political terms as the restoration of order within the state. The dominant feature of these turbulent and absorbing plays is their vitality, and the source of this dramatic energy must be sought in their author's excited concern with their central theme. In spite of the opportunities given by its subject-matter the tetralogy is not centred on either the usurped crown or the rivalry between a *de facto* king and a pretender with *de jure* rights; the characters from whom the springs of action come —Margaret and Richard of Gloucester in their dynamism and Henry in his quietism—would seek or shun power quite apart from the provocation given by York, who is of course motivated by dynastic ambition. It is the failure to observe 'degree' which leads

[1] The plays of Marlowe offer outstanding examples of Luciferian heroes, but they are fully developed creations in their own right and cannot safely be used to illustrate popular conceptions on which Shakespeare and his audience could intuitively draw.

first to faction in the commonwealth and finally to civil war. The conception of the false king becomes central only in the second tetralogy; in the first it is a genuine factor in the social confusion, but it is incidental, itself a result of an earlier breach of degree, rather than the cause of later ones. The statement of the theme is made in the opening scene of both Part I and Part II. The king is incapable of fulfilling his proper function since he cannot dominate the nobility of his realm, and the nobility in their self-seeking pride cannot unite to govern in his place while he is a child or to support him as a young man. In Part I this breakdown of order is declared to be the direct cause of the defeats in France:

> *Messenger*: Amongst the soldiers this is muttered,
>   That here you maintain several factions
>   And whilst a field should be dispatch'd and fought,
>   You are disputing of your generals: I, i, 70–3

Later it is the internecine rivalry between York and Somerset which reduces the gallant and disinterested Talbot to impotence and finally causes his death in the French wars. In Part II Duke Humphrey—the equivalent in this play of Talbot in the first, that is, the one honest man by whom the others must be judged—is first made powerless and then murdered by a faction of men who unite only until he is destroyed and then attack each other. In Part III the Yorkist faction itself splits and reopens the civil war: Warwick and Clarence were both good Yorkists until they thought it would pay them to be otherwise, just as York had earlier allied himself with the Lancastrians, Beaufort and Somerset, to gain his own ends. These divisions are quite independent of the weakness of Henry's title or of Edward's. They stem from the failure of men to fulfil their proper roles, and this failure spreads downwards through society like a rot until fathers and sons murder each other without knowing why, and men believe that seven half-penny loaves can be had for a penny and that three-hooped pots have ten hoops.[1]

The horror of disorder is nowhere more passionately presented than in the Talbot scenes of *1 Henry VI*. The most vivid lines are

---

[1] See *3 Henry VI*, II, v and *2 Henry VI*, IV, ii.

Somerset's; they show a vigorous speech-rhythm within the blank verse structure which is remarkable at so early a date.

> *Somerset*: York set him on; York should have sent him aid.
> *Lucy*: And York as fast upon your grace exclaims;
> Swearing that you withhold his levied host,
> Collected for this expedition.
> *Somerset*: York lies; he might have sent and had the horse;
> I owe him little duty, and less love;
> And take foul scorn to fawn on him by sending. IV, iv, 29–35

The scene between the doomed father and son begins with as solemn music as the last act of *Romeo and Juliet*.

> *Talbot*: But, O malignant and ill-boding stars!
> Now thou art come unto a feast of death,
> A terrible and unavoided danger:
> *1 Henry VI*, IV, v, 6–8

The material is admirably suited to Shakespeare's purpose of demonstrating the disastrous results of disunity in the commonwealth, and the visual picture of the dying father with the dead son in his arms at the climax of the episode is as clearly a foretaste of his later dramaturgy as is the blank verse at the opening.[1] It is interesting that in reading the second meeting between the father and son, that on the field of battle, appears no stronger in dramatic tension than the first, whereas on the stage the violent physical action of the fighting indicated by stage direction in the Folio was undoubtedly sufficient to overcome any tendency to flatness.

> *Alarum: excursions, wherein Talbot's Son is hemmed about, and Talbot rescues him.* IV, vi

The moral of the whole episode is voiced by York's messenger in a soliloquy of direct address to the audience:

> *Lucy*: Thus, while the vulture of sedition
> Feeds in the bosom of such great commanders,
> Sleeping neglection doth betray to loss
> The conquest of our scarce cold conqueror . . .

[1] Cf. for example, the last entry of King Lear and the duel between Edgar and Edmund.

THE LUCIFERIAN SIN: REBELLION

> Henry the Fifth: whiles they each other cross,
> Lives, honours, lands and all hurry to loss. IV, iii, 47–53

It is significant that Queen Margaret's contribution to the turmoil begins before there is any threat to the Lancastrian title. Her role is not that of a courageous woman daring everything to protect the threatened rights of husband or son, but of one who breaks the order appointed by divine law for womankind. In the first place she is unfaithful to her husband, and this breach of the moral order directly contributes to civil disorder through the jealousy of her favourite Suffolk shown by his rival peers. This is clearly her first sin, but it is treated in the play in a curious way. It is usually maintained that no sympathy with adulterous love is ever shown in Shakespeare except in the ambiguous case of Antony and Cleopatra. His early picture of Margaret and Suffolk is the single clear exception to this generalisation. Margaret is a portentous figure because she brings unusual strength to her evil purposes; she brings the same strength to her passion, and Suffolk reciprocates it. At their farewell—the first passionate love-scene Shakespeare wrote—there are the rhythms of true grief and of true love.

> *Margaret*: Go; speak not to me; even now be gone.
> O, go not yet! Even thus two friends condemn'd
> Embrace and kiss and take ten thousand leaves,
> Loather a hundred times to part than die.
> Yet now farewell; and farewell life with thee![1]
>
> 2 *Henry VI*, III, ii, 352–6

Suffolk, an aggressive bully elsewhere in the play, is given in this scene notes of Romeo's own music.

> *Suffolk*: Well could I curse away a winter's night,
> Though standing naked on a mountain top, . . .
> And think it but a minute spent in sport. . . .
> For where thou art, there is the world itself,

---

[1] Cf. *Juliet*: Wilt thou be gone? It is not yet near day . . .
  Therefore stay yet; thou need'st not to be gone. . . .
  Then, window, let day in, and let life out.
  Romeo: Farewell, farewell! one kiss and I'll descend.
  Romeo and Juliet, III, v, 1, 16, 41–2

With every several pleasure in the world,
And where thou art not, desolation.
I can no more.[1]   III, ii, 335–65

The sympathy for the lovers betrayed by some of those cadences
is of course contradictory to the playwright's attitude towards
them in their principal roles of disruptors of order and degree, and
possibly this is the first example of Shakespeare's concern with an
individual character slightly interfering with his shaping of the
play as a whole.

Margaret—to return to her significant function—is further
guilty in her attempt to rule the state in the place of the husband
whose proper duty this is. Suffolk promises her that after Humphrey's fall:

You yourself shall steer the happy helm.   I, iii, 96

But he is proffering a thing wrong as well as impossible. When
Margaret does in fact steer unaided it is to disaster. On the plain
of Tewkesbury she first bitterly condemns her husband and then
claims his place herself.

Yet lives our pilot still: Is't meet that he
Should leave the helm and like a fearful lad
With tearful eyes add water to the sea
And give more strength to that which hath too much,
Whiles, in his moan, the ship splits on the rock,
Which industry and courage might have saved?
Ah, what a shame! ah, what a fault were this! . . .
Why, is not Oxford here another anchor?
And Somerset another goodly mast?
The friends of France our shrouds and tacklings?
And, though unskilful, why not Ned and I

---

[1] Cf. *Romeo*: Night's candles are burnt out, and jocund day
Stands tiptoe on the misty mountain tops.   III, v, 9–10

There is no world without Verona walls . . .
                              heaven is here
Where Juliet lives; and every cat and dog
And little mouse, every unworthy thing
Live here in heaven and may look on her;
But Romeo may not.   III, iii, 3–33

19

For once allowed the skilful pilot's charge?

3 Henry VI, v, iv, 6–20

The wanton and hopeless challenge to superior forces which follows ensures the murders of both son and husband. Her ambition to rule had grown by the measure of success she had for a time achieved, and before provoking the battle at Tewkesbury she had broken the compromise between Henry and York which would have prevented its occasion.

Finally, Margaret not only fights but kills, and she herself inaugurates the terrible pattern of murder for vengeance which makes the end of her story so horrific. She has already instigated the murder of Humphrey, but in his case there was at least the hypocritical decency of concealment. The murder of York is openly gang vengeance in lieu of justice, and she takes part in it herself:

> *Margaret*: What, weeping-ripe, my Lord Northumberland?
> Think but upon the wrong he did us all . . .
> *Clifford*: Here's for my oath, here's for my father's death.
> [*stabbing him*
> *Margaret*: And here's to right our gentle-hearted king.
> [*stabbing him*
> I, iv, 172–6

The principal contribution to the disasters of his reign is however Henry's own. Unlike Margaret he makes no violent breaches in the social order; his sin is the negative one of refusing the responsibility his 'degree' cast upon him. Its first occasion is his failure to afford the justice and protection due to his Uncle, Gloucester, when he was falsely accused by his rival peers.

> My lord of Gloucester, 'tis my special hope
> That you will clear yourself from all suspect:
> My conscience tells me you are innocent.
> *2 Henry VI*, III, i, 139–41

In spite of his belief, however, he allows his own kingly power to be used by Gloucester's enemies for his destruction.

> My lords, what to your wisdoms seemeth best,
> Do or undo, as if ourself were here.   III, i, 195–6

Henry does not simply refuse to exercise judgment in a neutral case but refuses to make the effort necessary to implement the knowledge of his conscience that the arrested man is innocent.

He repeats this characteristic behaviour on another occasion. In the dispute with York in the Parliament House[1] he admits the legitimacy of York's claim before suggesting the compromise by which he makes York his heir. This is morally acceptable because it saves York from the sin of rebellion against his anointed king while at the same time admitting his own just claims. But once more Henry fails to exert his royal power to enforce a solution which he knows to be right. Weakly he tries to avoid facing his wife, and when this is impossible he pleads the coward's excuse:

> Pardon me, Margaret; pardon me, sweet son;
> The Earl of Warwick and the duke enforced me.
>
> 3 Henry VI, I, i, 228–9

His only attempt to check her appeal to force is the line she ignores:

> Stay, gentle Margaret, and hear me speak.   I, i, 257

Though he does not follow her to war, he does not disown the hope she may be successful.

> Revenged may she be on that hateful duke,
> Whose haughty spirit, winged with desire,
> Will cost my crown.   I, i, 265–7

Similarly, although he is not present at the battle of Wakefield nor before the fatal molehill on which York is murdered, he again accepts passively the fruits of deeds which he should, as king, have prevented.

The chaotic situation caused by the failure of the nobility, the queen and the king to observe 'degree' is particularly fraught with peril, however, because of the seizure of the throne by Henry Bolingbroke two generations before, so that although the throne is Henry's by possession yet it is York's by inheritance. The fact of Henry IV's usurpation is implicit in the story, though it is not exploited dramatically. The scene which deals most directly with

---

[1] 3 *Henry VI*, I, i.

this situation is the first of *3 Henry VI*. The most important lines are these:

> *King Henry*: Henry the Fourth by conquest got the crown.
> *York*: 'Twas by rebellion against his king.
> *King Henry* [aside]: I know not what to say; my title's weak.
> . . . Art thou against us, Duke of Exeter?
> *Exeter*: His is the right, and therefore pardon me. . . .
> My conscience tells me he is lawful king. . . .
> *Clifford*: King Henry, be thy title right or wrong,
> Lord Clifford vows to fight in thy defence:
> May the ground gape and swallow me alive,
> Where I shall kneel to him that slew my father!   I, i, 132–62

Here the contrasted reasons for Clifford's and Exeter's allegiance respectively to Lancaster and York clearly confirm Henry's own admission. Very little emotional play is made of this, however, so that the suggested compromise, which leaves the crowned king to reign during his life, breaks down finally only because the protagonists have a will to division and self-assertion and no will to peace.

In a similar way, although the legitimacy of his claim is stressed, the dramatist invites no particular sympathy for Edward IV at his accession. The rejoicing is confined to the three fierce brothers; dramatically the situation is 'thrown away'. Edward's first appearance after his coronation shows his undignified courtship of Lady Grey; the second of any length shows his share in the murder of the young Prince of Wales. Edward is certainly no glamorous hero returned at last to the throne of his fathers; beside his brother he foreshows already the weak and decadent figure-head he is to become in *Richard III*.

Indeed, far from offering any legal or logical reasons for the civil war, the emotional tone of the play is dependent upon the utter senselessness of its tragedy. This receives its most emphatic expression at Towton. After the battle, the son who has killed his father mourns:

> Pardon me, God, I knew not what I did!   II, v, 69

The father who has killed his son is equally ignorant of any purpose behind his act, and the king himself denies the validity of the cause in which the soldiers so unnaturally fight; in face of their grief he can only say:

> Woe above woe! grief more than common grief! . . .
> Wither one rose, and let the other flourish;
> If you contend, a thousand lives must wither.   II, v, 94–102

The 'deadly quarrel' is in no good cause. What matter who reigns, provided the slaughter be stopped? In fact, so unimportant to Shakespeare's mind at this time were the dynastic rights and wrongs of the situation, that the audience's point of view about them is manœuvred by blatantly playing off sympathy for and against the individuals concerned. Margaret, the foreigner, the adulteress, the man-woman, must always be condemned, and whenever we see him unkingly in action, so must Henry. In conflict with them York appears the wronged victim, but when the Yorkist king is the 'machiavel', Richard, it is equally easy to ensure sympathy for the murdered Henry, so that at the end of the play Derby can declare, as he offers Richard's crown to Richmond:

> Lo, here, this long-usurped royalty
> From the dead temples of this bloody wretch
> Have I pluck'd off, to grace thy brows withal:
> > *Richard III*, v, v, 4–6

'Long-usurped' cannot apply to Richard's recent seizing of the crown from his nephew, but must refer to his family's rebellion against Henry VI. What is dramatically important is not that the dynasty has been changed, but that wickedness has been punished and peace restored by the Tudor king. We are emotionally interested not in the righting of an ancient wrong but in the future prospect of unity and prosperity.

> *Richmond*: England hath long been mad, and scarr'd herself;
> The brother blindly shed the brother's blood,
> The father rashly slaughter'd his own son,
> The son, compell'd, been butcher to the sire: . . .
> O, now, let Richmond and Elizabeth,

The true succeeders of each royal house,
By God's fair ordinance conjoin together!
And let their heirs, God, if thy will be so,
Enrich the time to come with smooth-faced peace,
With smiling plenty and fair prosperous days!   v, v, 23–34

The play *Richard III*, therefore, completes the dramatic pattern
begun with *1 Henry VI* and consistently developed. The four plays
embody a single situation in which, by a classical peripeteia, violence breeds its own destruction, and together they are able to state
unequivocally this single basic theme.

In this, his first treatment of English history, Shakespeare was
content to follow the orthodox thought of the time. He deals
primarily with the sins of social disorder, and in so far as he is concerned with justice his play points out the simple truth that he who
draws the sword perishes by the sword. Queen Margaret's words
to her deposed successor emphasise the exactness of the price to be
paid.

> I had an Edward, till a Richard kill'd him;
> I had a Harry, till a Richard kill'd him:
> Thou hadst an Edward, till a Richard kill'd him;
> Thou hadst a Richard, till a Richard kill'd him....
> Thy Edward he is dead, that stabb'd my Edward;
> Thy other Edward dead, to quit my Edward;
> Young York he is but boot, because both they
> Match not the high perfection of my loss.   iv, iv, 40–66

The intense pity for human suffering which the plays express is
Shakespeare's personal contribution to his material. It is as clear in
the stylised verse telling of the griefs of father and son at Towton,
as it is in the lament of young Clifford, where there is a pre-echo of
the music of Cordelia's voice:

> *Clifford*: ...Wast thou ordain'd, dear father,
> To lose thy youth in peace, and to achieve
> The silver livery of advised age,
> And, in thy reverence and thy chair-days, thus
> To die in ruffian battle?
>
> *2 Henry VI*, v, ii, 45–9

This tenderness never disappears, and it has much to do with the values accepted or discarded when Shakespeare came to write his more mature panorama of English history.

As Shakespeare finished writing *Richard III*, he must have found, however, that his thought was already running along somewhat different tracks and turning to concepts which sought expression rather in religious than in political terms. When Richard awoke screaming:

> Have mercy, Jesu!—Soft! I did but dream.
>
> *Richard III*, v, iii, 178

he is every guilty man rather than a particular guilty king. His sin springs from man's universal desire to defy the limits appointed him in his creation, and since this could no longer be dramatised on the English stage in theological terms, Shakespeare continued to use the political symbol of *hubris*—the defiance of the king, rather than its religious equivalent—the defiance of God. When he returns to the epic of York and Lancaster his emphasis is no longer on general disruption. His interest has turned to the individual's original sin; he states it in the traditional terms of usurping a throne and goes on to dramatise the proliferating fruits of such an act in the hopes, fears and agonies of particular men and women. Beside this fascinated observation of the apparently inevitable results of wrongdoing there now appears in the plays an equally strong— even obsessional—interest in the search for a way of escape from the circle, a source of mercy for the offender. At first these two streams of thought appear to flow independently and are only visible in different plays, but when the moment of *King Lear* arrives their waters come together at last in a single magnificent flood. Before this point is reached, however, it is necessary to consider the shift of emphasis by which Shakespeare's thought moves away from the general breach of degree to the specific defiance of the king. This new interest is what distinguishes the structure of the second historical tetralogy from that of the first.

3. THE USURPED THRONE

Richard II; *Henry IV*; *Henry V*; *Macbeth*; *Julius Caesar*

It is pleasant to imagine that Shakespeare at the age of eleven actually witnessed the performance of the Coventry Cycle which took place at Kenilworth in 1575.[1]

> *Lucifer*: I wyl go sythen in Goddes seat
> Above sunne and mone and starres or sky
> I am now set as ye may see
> Now worship me for most mighty
> And for your lord honour now me
> Syttyng in my seat.
> *Deus*: Thou Lucyfer ffor thi mekyl pride
> I byode thee fall from heaven to hell...
> At my commandment anoon down thou slyde
> With mirth and joy never more to mell.
> *Lucifer*: At thy bidding this syl I werke
> And pas from joy to peyne smerte
> Now I am a devil full darke
> That was an angelle bryht.[2]

If he had never heard similar words on a stage, there is no doubt of the power of their story over his imagination, for he dramatised such blind and arrogant rebellion against the divine purpose, not once but many times, in terms of the illicit assumption of a throne. Apparently this symbol was already burning in his imagination at the end of *3 Henry VI*, but it was too late then to incorporate it as the centre of interest, for this was already fixed elsewhere. The mind of the king-killer is never more vividly revealed than it is in Richard of Gloucester, but his murder of Henry VI is only one incident in the pattern of civil strife and does not appear as more important to Richard himself than his other murders. The later plays, however, show that it *was* more important to Shakespeare, and Richard will be considered later among the other killers of a king.

---

[1] Civic records show that the Coventry plays were 'laid down' in 1580.
[2] This is the text of the *Ludus Coventriae* play. The MS. of the Coventry Guild play is of course lost.

In *Richard II* the divine pattern is so suggested as to win our acceptance of its fitness, but this is done principally by the poetry which describes it or alludes to it, for we never see in existence the ordered Kingdom ruled with justice and mercy in accord with the purposes of God. The chorus-like figures of the gardeners, who are related to this play as the equally anonymous Father and Son are to *Henry VI*, make the comparison of state and garden in a style as formal as that of the Elizabethan knot and herb gardens which they praise.

> *Gardener*: Cut off the heads of too fast growing sprays,
> That look too lofty in our commonwealth:
> All must be even in our government....
> *Servant*: Why should we in the compass of a pale
> Keep law and form and due proportion,
> Showing, as in a model, our firm estate,
> When our sea-walled garden, the whole land,
> Is full of weeds...
> Her knots disordered and her wholesome herbs
> Swarming with caterpillars? III, iv, 34–47

Richard himself does not conform to the pattern; that is both his sin and his tragedy, and the divine purpose is once again thwarted as it had been in that earlier garden of our first parents. The Commonwealth, thus first betrayed from within by the man who frivolously left empty the place he had been divinely deputed to fill, was defenceless before the external attack of Bolingbroke, who by fraud and force defeated and murdered his anointed sovereign. It is true that it was Piers Exton's hands that actually shed Richard's blood, and that Bolingbroke allowed Northumberland, that 'haught insulting man', to do much of his bullying for him, but he is none the more acceptable for that, and this 'silent king', who was clever enough to wait while his rival walked into the net spread for him, is clearly himself responsible for the 'trenching war' and 'the intestine shock and furious close of civil butchery', which he laments at the beginning of the next play. It is not long before we are reminded of his victim, for the forceful dissyllable of his name occurs three times in thirty lines of Act I, scene iii.

Worcester: I cannot blame him: was not he proclaim'd
By Richard that dead is the next of blood?...
Hotspur: But, soft, I pray you; did King Richard then
Proclaim my brother Edmund Mortimer
Heir to the crown?...
Shall it for shame be spoken in these days,...
That men of your nobility and power
Did gage them both in an unjust behalf,...
To put down Richard, that sweet lovely rose,
And plant this thorn, this canker, Bolingbroke?

1 Henry IV, I, iii, 145–76

It is accompanied by the name of the rightful heir which is hammered into the ear fourteen times before the scene ends. We hear of noble Mortimer, revolted Mortimer, foolish Mortimer, downtrod Mortimer, until Hotspur seems to have become the very starling he would have taught to 'speak nothing but "Mortimer"', to keep the king's 'anger still in motion'.

The crime of the first play is thus brought right to the centre of the attention and nailed there firmly at the start of the second. This is important, for the origin of the rebellion of the northern lords soon loses its prominence. If it were clearly developed the rebels would inevitably become the heroes of the play, and this no dramatist could afford to allow in the 1590's. Yet it is the logic of the situation. It was potent in Shakespeare's imagination and it leads to a curious and increasing ambivalence in his work which reaches its peak in the character of Henry V.

We have already noticed Shakespeare's surprising ability to be a voice for a discredited minority, but in his first presentation of the rebels he does not emphasise the legitimacy of their cause. When Hotspur and his allies define their aims (*1 Henry IV*, III, i) they do not mention the restoration of the Yorkist line but only the division of England into three estates for themselves. In this they commit a fault close to Richard's own when he leased his revenues and turned his realm into a 'tenement or pelting farm'. Later indeed Hotspur does put forward their claims as representatives of the disinherited Earl of March, and vividly recapitulates Henry's treachery

28

to Richard, but here again Shakespeare does not leave the rebels' cause unsmeared. The Earl of Worcester warns Hotspur:

> ...stop all sight-holes, every loop from whence
> The eye of reason may pry in upon us:
> This absence of your father's draws a curtain,
> That shows the ignorant a kind of fear
> Before not dreamt of.
>   IV, i, 71–5

The imagery here is as threatening and dark as Lady Macbeth's when she faces for a moment the full implications of her fell purpose:

> Come, thick night,
> And pall thee in the dunnest smoke of hell,
> That my keen knife see not the wound it makes,
> Nor heaven peep through the blanket of the dark,
> To cry 'Hold, hold.'
>   *Macbeth*, I, v, 51–5

The extreme vividness and superficial incongruity of the images of the peepholes in the blanket and the curtain hanging limply from its rings show that for Shakespeare the association of hanging drapery with secret evil must have been very strong and reinforces the suggestion that in Worcester's words the rebels themselves are made to suggest the wrongness of their action. Facing the Northern lords, Prince John voices the claims of the reigning family with force and dignity:

> You have ta'en up,
> Under the counterfeited zeal of God,
> The subjects of his substitute, my father,
> And both against the peace of heaven and him
> Have here up-swarm'd them.
>   *2 Henry IV*, IV, ii, 26–30

But the substitute of this substitute of God shortly afterwards perpetrates the most cold-blooded treachery in Gaultree Forest, and Shakespeare adapts his source in order to give the treachery to a member of the royal house itself. In spite of Worcester's words the balance of sympathy here is clearly with the rebels, not with the prince. Something seems to be compelling Shakespeare to cloud the issue, and indeed the Tudor horror of rebellion is obviously at work in the play, muddying the clarity of its design. Shakespeare never forgets, however, the origin of these dilemmas and this is clear from the fact that he never allows Henry himself to forget that the primary cause of all his misfortunes—and ironically of other men's sins if rebellion against him be a sin—is his own action. He says to his son:

> I know not whether God will have it so...
> But thou dost in thy passages of life
> Make me believe that thou art only mark'd
> For the hot vengeance and the rod of heaven
> To punish my mistreadings.

> *1 Henry IV*, III, ii, 4–11

He is haunted by the memory of the past; indeed there is no play where more brilliant vignettes of past scenes are conjured up, often by Henry, although sometimes by the rebels too. Again and again the past intrudes on the present. Henry makes for himself the excuse of necessity, but he always sees himself and his past in terms of a guilt the Dead-Sea fruits of which he finally admits:

> ...But which of you was by?—
> You, cousin Nevil, as I may remember—
> When Richard, with his eye brimful of tears,
> Then check'd and rated by Northumberland,
> Did speak these words, now proved a prophecy!
> 'Northumberland, thou ladder by the which
> My cousin Bolingbroke ascends my throne,'
> Though then, God knows, I had no such intent,
> But that necessity so bow'd the state
> That I and greatness were compelled to kiss;
> 'The time shall come', thus did he follow it,
> 'The time will come, that foul sin, gathering head,
> Shall break into corruption': so went on,
> Foretelling this same time's condition,
> And the division of our amity.

> *2 Henry IV*, III, i, 65–79

He winces at a hint of his past by others, as when, in his hasty interruption of Northumberland he covers his pain by an outburst of temper.

> *Worcester*: Our house, my sovereign liege, little deserves
> The scourge of greatness to be used on it;
> And that same greatness too which our own hands
> Have holp to make so portly.
> *North.*: My lord,—
> *K. Henry*: Worcester, get thee gone;...
> You have good leave to leave us: when we need
> Your use and counsel, we shall send for you.
>
> *1 Henry IV*, I, iii, 10–21

In case it be felt that the unity suggested by these continuous references to the past extends only to the first three plays, it should be remembered that the last of them occurs in the mouth of Henry V on the eve of Agincourt. It is the force with which the plays present the passage of time during which a single evil deed prolongs its influence and proliferates in unforeseen directions that makes this tetralogy so impressive as a whole, for the space it provides is used dramatically in working out to the full the implications of its theme.

At the opening of *1 Henry IV* we see the loyalty of men like Blunt beginning to attach itself sincerely to the new king, but the pattern is continually flawed or broken by the old evil, and there is a curiously moving scene at Shrewsbury when the Douglas dispatches one simulacrum after another and finds no certainly true king, even when he at last encounters Henry himself.

> *Douglas*: ...what art thou,
> That counterfeit'st the person of a king?
> *Henry*: The king himself; who, Douglas, grieves at heart,
> So many of his shadows thou hast met
> And not the very king...
> *Douglas*: I fear thou art another counterfeit. v, iv, 27–35

But can it finally be claimed that the theme of regicide and its consequences unfolded in the first three plays does in fact inform *Henry V*? I believe that it can, although the pattern is obscured by an ambiguity at the heart of the fourth play, which has led to different opinions about the basic design of the tetralogy. In his Festival production of 1951, Anthony Quayle sought its unity in the gradual 'grooming' of the Prince of Wales into England's ideal king. This attempt failed because it involved transmogrifying three characters —Richard and Bolingbroke as well as Hal himself—by frequent playing against the sense of Shakespeare's lines. We saw in Bolingbroke a modest and serene young rebel, facing a degenerate and ultimately worthless king, and this is not an accurate presentation of the relationship Shakespeare created between Richard and his successor. The play's pattern does not show Hal's development into Shakespeare's ideal monarch: it shows rather the impossibility that the murdered Richard could ever be forgotten or peace and prosperity ever arise out of bloodshed.

This interpretation is enforced by the closest of the links between the plots of *2 Henry IV* and *Henry V*. The last speech of the first play is Prince John's, and contains the lines:

> I will lay odds that, ere this year expire,
> We bear our civil swords and native fire
> As far as France.
>
> V, V, 111–13

To distract men's thoughts from his doubtful title by foreign conquest was Henry IV's dying advice to his son, and to follow this advice is the son's first major decision of policy after ascending the throne. It seems impossible not to believe that Shakespeare was deliberately ambiguous here. When *Henry V* is performed by itself it is possible to interpret Henry as sincerely anxious to establish his rightful title to the French crown before declaring war and as genuinely convinced by the archbishop's deliberately tendentious reasoning. But when the earlier play is remembered his motives must be suspect. We know his father had considered even the rewinning of the Holy Sepulchre as a means of securing his own usurped throne. He admits he

> had a purpose now
> To lead out many to the Holy Land,
> Lest rest and lying still might make them look
> Too near unto my state. Therefore, my Harry,

> Be it thy course to busy giddy minds
> With foreign quarrels.

2 Henry IV, IV, v, 210–15

Such 'machiavellism' cannot possibly have been intended to win approval, yet it is in principle identical with Henry V's later conduct. The audience forgets happily enough their hero's hidden motive, and probably Shakespeare intended that they should, but he himself when writing the play can hardly have done so, and his knowledge throws an additional irony into the famous lines of Michael Williams:

Bates: We know enough, if we know we are the king's subjects: if his cause be wrong, our obedience to the king wipes the crime of it out of us.

Williams: But if the cause be not good, the king himself hath a heavy reckoning to make, when all those legs and arms and heads, chopped off in a battle, shall join together at the latter day and cry all 'We died at such a place'; some swearing, some crying for a surgeon, some upon their wives left poor behind them, some upon the debts they owe, some upon their children rawly left. I am afeared there are few die well that die in a battle; for how can they charitably dispose of any thing, when blood is their argument? Now, if these men do not die well, it will be a black matter for the king that led them to it; whom to disobey were against all proportion of subjection.

Henry V, IV, i, 130–46

Richard's murder followed by the wars in France is really as clear an example of violence breeding violence as any that *Macbeth* itself can show, and by Henry's agonised prayer before the battle, Agincourt is indissolubly linked to Pomfret.

> Not to-day, O Lord,
> O, not to-day, think not upon the fault
> My father made in compassing the crown!

IV, i, 310–12

Henry V fails as completely as do his father and his son to give his people the peace which is the intended and decorous pattern of social life, and the direct reason of the failure of all three men lies in their wrongful title to the throne, which accounts for the foreign wars in the one reign as completely as it does for the civil wars in the next.

Like his father, like Claudius, like Macbeth even, Henry V succeeded in establishing a temporary order on an unsound foundation, but in spite of its glamour it was as spurious as the ceremonial of Claudius' stately court or Macbeth's ghost-haunted banquet—a mere mockery of the god-given order which had been violated. The price of Henry IV's rebellion was paid in full not by himself or his son but by his grandson and the people of his realm, and this Shakespeare must have remembered when he wrote of the wooing of Katharine.

Shall not thou and I, between Saint Denis and Saint George, compound a boy, half French, half English, that shall go to Constantinople and take the Turk by the beard? shall we not? what sayest thou, my fair flower-de-luce?   v, ii, 219-24

It was a hope that was soon to be belied.

Before the embarkation for France there is a similar though smaller example of the equivocal treatment of historical material to which Shakespeare was driven in this play. Considered only in the setting of *Henry V* the motive for the treachery of Cambridge, Scroop and Grey is quite without importance, at least for the normal playgoer whose whole attention is focused on the heroic figure of the threatened king, while the traitors themselves are made peculiarly repulsive by their hypocritical calls for vengeance on the drunkard whom the king forgives. But in the light of the plays of *Henry VI*—already written by Shakespeare—it is evident that the three men represent the cause of the murdered Richard. The dramatist himself cannot conceivably have been unaware of the fact, for in his own—or at the very least his company's—earlier play, these words are spoken by Earl Mortimer to Richard of York:

> Long after this, when Henry the Fifth,
> Succeeding his father Bolingbroke did reign,
> Thy father, Earl of Cambridge, then derived
> From famous Edmund Langley, Duke of York...
> Levied an army, weening to redeem

And have install'd me in the diadem:
But, as the rest, so fell that noble earl
And was beheaded.

1 Henry VI, II, v, 82–91

In as recent a play as *1 Henry IV* Shakespeare had made the Arch-bishop of York send a sealed letter[1] 'to my cousin Scroop' to sum-mon him to the Yorkist forces.[2] This man also was sent to his death by Henry for his support of the Earl of Cambridge, whose son suc-cessfully asserted his claim to the throne against Henry's son in the Parliament House some thirty years later. No word of all this is uttered in defence of the rebels in *Henry V*, but that they *had* a de-fence, the dramatist very well knew; it was, however, one which no patriotic Elizabethan, lost in admiration of the usurper's son, would care to hear.

Although the two historical tetralogies were created indepen-dently of each other this does not mean that Shakespeare was ob-livious of Bosworth as he wrote of earlier happenings; on the con-trary he appears, very naturally, to have been increasingly aware of the shadow of coming events as he approached the end of *Henry V*, and this awareness must have brought him a measure of satisfaction. It perhaps appeared to him that if the original *hubris* could ever be forgiven it would be in the case of the modest victor of Agincourt. But he allows no escape; the wages could only be postponed not remitted, and it is possible that in the dramatist's view the child of Henry and Katharine fulfilled his destiny when, instead of taking the Turk by the beard at Constantinople as his father had hoped, he died in the Tower, a vicarious sacrifice, that the sins of his grand-father might be atoned.

Shakespeare's material dictated to him a triumph for Henry V which should include not only military victory but a full measure of admiring affection for this 'star of England'. Equally his material

---

[1] *1 Henry IV*, IV, iv.

[2] The Scroop executed by Henry was in fact the nephew of the archbishop. There is no reference to him in Holinshed in connection with the rebels, and he is not known to have been implicated in the northern rebellion. I can find no other historical character to whom Shakespeare could have been referring however, and his choice of the name is therefore significant.

35

dictated—in his view—condemnation and failure for the archetypal rebel, the king-murderer. Within the framework of the second tetralogy these two purposes are mutually exclusive, but the history of their own land assured both dramatist and audience that, while they could love their hero-king, yet they were assured of the fulfilment of the pattern of justice which they had been long taught to expect in the events of the world.

It is clear that, although considerable licence to tamper with his sources, particularly by omission, evidently existed for the Elizabethan dramatist, the material of English history became increasingly unmalleable for Shakespeare's purposes. Rich in themes he seized on as fertile, these stories of the kings of England could not be exploited so as to externalise what was to the dramatist their full significance. The implications of this come increasingly from imagery and comment, such as Michael Williams's description of death in battle, rather than from the structure of outward events, which may indeed be in contradiction to them, as when Henry's guilt-ridden memories of Richard's murder occur just before the apparently 'crowning mercy' of Agincourt. To fulfil his imaginative purpose Shakespeare needed material which he could handle more freely; he soon found it.

Macbeth presents the most striking example of the restatement by Shakespeare of a theme left ambiguous in the history plays. Here Shakespeare returns to the subject of the usurper, and since he is able to shape his plot more freely it is valuable to discover in what ways *Macbeth*'s structure differs from that imposed by historical fact on the earlier plays. Each modification draws the characters closer to their Christian prototypes. In the first place Shakespeare adapts his story so as to take from Macbeth all genuine grievances against the king such as were prominent in the case of Bolinbroke. He selects and arranges his material to ensure that the murdered king is wholly attractive, unlike Richard II or Henry VI, and also gives him worthy heirs of age to rule; for although Malcolm was young, he was—unlike the children of Edward IV—old enough to fight in battle as well as to be declared Prince of Cumberland. He allows Macbeth also a full measure of the popularity, reputation, honour, charm and also the happiness in marriage which were denied to Richard III. Like Lucifer's, and indeed Adam's, his rebellion lacks any motive other than the rebel's own self-assertion.

The play also develops the figure of the Saviour prince more fully than was possible in the English history plays. Richmond is simply introduced as a child blessed by Henry VI, but Malcolm is not only more developed as a character; he is the eldest son of the king, and the declaration that he is his father's heir is what directly precipitates Macbeth's treachery. This situation is not used in the miracle plays of Lucifer's rebellion, but it was well known to legend, and Shakespeare is not the only poet to appreciate its dramatic value.

> Hear all ye Angels, Progenie of Light, ...
> This day have I begot whom I declare
> My onely Son ...
>   your Head I him appoint;
> And by myself have sworn to him shall bow
> All knees in Heav'n, and shall confess him Lord
>   *Paradise Lost*, v, ll. 600 ff.

In Macbeth, moreover, the role of Lucifer is conflated with that of Herod, for when the king's heir has escaped his clutches the tyrant seeks and finds a substitute victim. The outrage of innocence, symbolised by the murder of a child, is an important element in Shakespeare's thought, and here history presented the dramatist with only too much of the material he needed. But the killing of the young Macduff is peculiarly brutal because it is of no possible use to Macbeth; in committing this act he is baser even than his biblical forerunner, for he knew the life he wanted to take was safe from him, and he murdered from mere hysterical vindictiveness.

Finally, there is in *Macbeth* a new and more potent use of the supernatural. The history plays had, of course, touched on such material in varying ways. In *Henry VI* witchcraft had blackened La Pucelle in the eyes of her audience, and conjuring was fully integrated into the plot when the accusations against his wife were used by Gloucester's enemies to ensure his downfall. In *Richard III*, the visible dreams of the rival leaders had demonstrated the characteristically ambiguous method by which Shakespeare presents events in such a way that they may be interpreted either metaphysically or naturalistically, at the spectator's choice. There were, however, few places in the history plays where such a suggestion of supernatural influence on the human situation could be made of structural importance to the plot, whereas in *Macbeth* Shakespeare was able to achieve this and so to screw up to an unusual pitch the tension between predestination and freewill which is so marked a feature of the play. In such ways as these Shakespeare is allowing his work to approximate more closely than before to the old story of Lucifer and the Lord, and although his concern with the values of absolute Good and Evil is embodied in characters of excelling individuality and realism, yet the play's implications are universal.

> *Malcolm*: Comes the king forth, I pray you?
> *Doctor*: Ay, sir; There are a crew of wretched souls
> That stay his cure: their malady convinces
> The great assay of art; but at his touch—
> Such sanctity hath heaven given his hand—
> They presently amend....
> *Macduff*: What's the disease he means?
> *Malcolm*: 'Tis call'd the evil:
>
> IV, iii, 140-7

The word is all-inclusive.

There is another play which clearly deals with an attack on a throne; this is *Julius Caesar*. Its likeness to the plays we have been considering is deceptive, however, and is dependent on superficial resemblances of subject-matter only. Its story of murder and 'justice' demands some consideration at this point of our study, but the play's imaginative centre will, it is believed, be found to lie elsewhere. *Julius Caesar* can be presented either as a Roman version of the sin of king-killing or as a vindication of egalitarianism, and theatrical production can swing it to either pattern. The story appears to move in the clear daylight of the classical world with its characters distanced in their pagan civilisation and untrammelled by either the mystic illumination or the haunting guilt of a later age.

Certainly the verse has a limpid clarity rarely equalled, yet in spite of this, and of its vivid characterisation and the clean lines of its plot, the drama achieves no definitive statement. On the contrary it is perhaps the most ambiguous of all Shakespeare's plays.

Even in Plutarch the story is equivocal. In North's translation of the *Life of Brutus* Shakespeare read:[1] 'It is also reported, that Brutus could evil away with the tyranny, and that Cassius hated the tyrant:... for Cassius, even from his cradle, could not abide any manner of tyrants.' Similarly, it is said that Ligarius hated Caesar 'for that he was brought in danger of his tyrannical power'. The word *liberty* moreover is several times used in contexts clearly implying approval: for example: ' "For myself then", said Brutus, "I mean not to hold my peace, but to withstand it, and rather die than lose my liberty." Cassius, being bold, and taking hold of this word: "Why", quoth he, "what Roman is he alive that will suffer thee to die for thy liberty?" '

The attack on Caesar is shown to be justifiable:

... when they had thus given him the bridle to grow to this greatness, and that they could not then pull him back, though indeed in sight it would turn one day to the destruction of the whole state and commonwealth of Rome: too late they found that there is not so little a beginning of anything, but continuance of time will soon make it strong.

Life of Julius Caesar

In spite of this Plutarch's narrative clearly attributes the failure of the rebellion to the fact that it was contrary to the divine will: Caesar's

... great prosperity and good fortune ... did continue afterwards in the revenge of his death, pursuing the murtherers both by sea and land, till they had not left a man to be executed, of all them that were actors or counsellers in the conspiracy of his death.... *But above all, the ghost that appeared unto Brutus showed plainly that the gods were offended with the murther of Caesar.*[2]

At the time that Shakespeare read this narrative he was deeply concerned with the problem of rebellion and its fruits, and he must

---

[1] *Shakespeare's Plutarch*, ed. by W. W. Skeat (Macmillan, 1875).
[2] Italics the author's.

have seen in this Roman material two figures who might qualify for what the homilist would have called the 'Luciferian' role. Caesar himself certainly aspired to a crown, though 'it was not a crown neither, it was one of those coronets'. Plutarch describes it as 'a laurel crown ... having a royal band or diadem wreathed about it, which in old time was the ancient mark or token of a king' (*Life of Antony*). In any case Caesar desired it, and Shakespeare certainly must have noticed that when Caesar had refused it a third time he 'commanded the crown to be carried unto Jupiter in the Capitol' (*Life of Julius Caesar*), presumably because such a symbol properly belonged there. Nevertheless, the throne Caesar desired was empty. He is an image of ambition certainly, but not of rebellion or disloyalty in any obvious way; he is also courageous, public-spirited and nowhere shown as tyrannical or cruel; he is certainly no Richard of Gloucester.

His henchman, Antony, is of a similar 'mingled yarn'; he is an opportunist if not a charlatan, but he is given the certain seal of the verse rhythms for the genuineness of his distress at Caesar's death:

> O mighty Caesar! dost thou lie so low?
> Are all thy conquests, glories, triumphs, spoils,
> Shrunk to this little measure?   III, i, 148–50

It is the same man, however, who cynically orders:

> Fetch the will hither, and we shall determine
> How to cut off some charge in legacies.   IV, i, 8–9

This is the avenger who carries dead Caesar's cause forward, and his partisans are the rabble, who leave a poet's body battered in the market-place only because his name is Cinna, and the laconic Octavius who finally destroys him.

A similar duality appears in the presentation of the principal conspirators. Brutus and Cassius may, like Caesar, be motivated by ambition, but they are like him also in that they betray no owed allegiance. In spite of this Shakespeare does seem to be adapting his source so as to endorse the medieval condemnation of Caesar's murderers.[1] Plutarch describes Brutus' vision thus:

---

[1] Cf. their position in Dante's *Inferno*.

Looking towards the light of the lamp that waxed very dim, he saw a horrible vision of a man, of a wonderful greatness and dreadful look, which at the first made him marvellously afraid...at length he asked him what he was. The image answered him: I am thy ill angel, Brutus, and thou shalt see me by the city of Phillippes.   *Life of Brutus*

Shakespeare, when he modified this account and made the spirit the ghost of Julius Caesar, must have known that such a personal ghost would suggest to his auditors the Christian implications of the 'revenge' plays.[1] A similar resonance sounds when Antony voices the revenge motif in his lament over Caesar's body:

> And Caesar's spirit, ranging for revenge,
> With Ate by his side come hot from hell,
> Shall in these confines with a monarch's voice
> Cry 'Havoc', and let slip the dogs of war.   III, i, 270–3

The ghost of Caesar with Ate by his side might well have been a figure in an Induction similar to that of *The Spanish Tragedy*, and it will be shown that the design of the 'revenge' play was itself symbolic of the working of the divine justice, which, in the person of the avenger, waited until the wicked man made the trap into which he blindly walked. This is exactly what Brutus does by his ill-judged decision to fight at Philippi. The decision is adequately motivated psychologically by Brutus' lack of judgment and Cassius' loyalty to his friend; nevertheless, the dramatic pattern here, as far as it is imaginatively apprehended by the audience, marks out Brutus and Cassius as the wrongdoers, punished by the divine forces in the universe for mortal sin.

But such an imaginative apprehension by the audience is just what Shakespeare refuses to leave unblurred in this fascinating play. Cassius manifests traits typical of the arch-rebel: his ambition is mentioned several times, and he takes delight in openly defying the divine powers. He also plays the role of the serpent when he tempts both Casca and Brutus to join the conspirators. Casca he wins by cunningly misinterpreting the divine purposes as they are shown in the supernatural events of the storm.

[1] See below, pp. 87 ff.

> You are dull, Casca,...
> But if you would consider the true cause...
> Why all these things change from their ordinance
> Their natures and preformed faculties
> To monstrous quality,—why, you shall find
> That heaven hath infused them with these spirits,
> To make them instruments of fear and warning
> Unto some monstrous state.   I, iii, 57–71

This is certainly Satanic strategy, but the treatment of Brutus is ambiguous. After Cassius has 'whetted' his friend against Caesar, he admits in his soliloquy that he has been urging him to do something which he himself considers to be wrong:

> therefore it is meet
> That noble minds keep ever with their likes;
> For who so firm that cannot be seduced?   I, ii, 314–16

We have just witnessed, that is to say, a 'temptation scene'. Since this is so, the position of Cassius' soliloquy becomes significant; the great dialogue between the two men has preceded it, and we have there listened to Cassius without any warning that his motives are suspect. On the contrary the rhythm and structure of the verse are such that immediate sympathy for him is ensured.

> Ay, and that tongue of his that bade the Romans
> Mark him and write his speeches in their books,
> Alas, it cried 'Give me some drink, Titinius,'
> As a sick girl.   I, ii, 124–7

The narrow vowels make the mimicry of the high, plaintive voice irresistibly ridiculous and by contrast reinforce the infectious vigour of what shortly follows:

> Why, man, he doth bestride the narrow world
> Like a Colossus, and we petty men
> Walk under his huge legs.   I, ii, 134–6

When Iago tempts Othello there is no possibility of misapprehension, for aside and soliloquy have revealed Iago *before* not *after* he attacks the virtue of his master. Cassius is allowed to make a favourable impression on us first. The secondary impression given by the soliloquy does not wipe out the earlier one and apparently was not designed to do so, for in the second part of the play every dramatic device is exploited to win sympathy for the conspirators, so that the last tributes to the dead leaders, by each other as well as by their opponents, are accepted without query at their face value.

Like that of Cassius the portrait of Brutus is also equivocal. Both before and after the assassination he suffers the sleeplessness typical of a troubled conscience, and his final epitome of the whole venture includes the eschatological metaphor:

> Our enemies have beat us to the pit.   v, v, 23

Nevertheless, he strives to be honest with himself and others; he is idealistic, a loving husband, an adored master. Indeed Brutus' true 'sin' is never wrongful self-assertion. Already perhaps Shakespeare was aware of some inadequacy to his purposes in the Luciferian myth on which he was depending. Man's *blindness* is the clue which leads to the central significance of *Julius Caesar*, and the play must therefore receive its final analysis among those concerned with false-seeming rather than with *hubris*.

CHAPTER II

THE CHARACTER OF THE USURPER

1. SOME TYPICAL FIGURES

Richard III; Henry IV; Macbeth; Claudius; Edmund

The compelling power of the Lucifer image is so marked that it becomes of interest to analyse the character of the men Shakespeare chooses to set before us as representatives of the arch-rebel. With the ambiguous figures of Henry V, Octavius, Brutus and Cassius set aside for separate consideration, there remains a homogeneous group with similar characteristics who all aspire to gain kingship by unlawful means, and who thus fulfil the familiar Luciferian role. In so doing they all deliberately 'take degree away, untune that string', and thus set loose for their own purposes forces of chaos entirely beyond their own control. Edmund, who is the most self-conscious and therefore articulate of them all, can legitimately be used in interpreting the others, for although he never achieves kingship he is clearly an aspirant to its power and very nearly a successful one. As the husband of either Goneril or Regan he would be king of half Britain, and if Albany's wife had successfully arranged her husband's 'taking off' Edmund would have been in a fair way to securing the absolute power he craved. Although Edmund declares:

> Thou, nature, art my goddess; to thy law
> My services are bound.
>
> *King Lear*, I, ii, 1-2

His conduct shows that in reality *he is bound to nothing* apart from his own desires, and that the only law he serves is his 'own appetite' with which he identifies Nature. To Edmund the bonds of blood are no more sacred than the bonds of allegiance. To him 'a credulous father . . . and a brother noble' are simply fair game, and the words in which he proclaims 'I will persevere in my course of loyalty, though the conflict be sore between that and my blood', are to him no more than counters, false coin which will serve to defraud a man as unscrupulous as himself.

Richard III vaunts a like independence and dispatches brother and nephew with equal gusto. Richard's character, drawn, of course, from the traditional Tudor orthodoxy concerning this Yorkist 'usurper', is developed consistently throughout the second and third parts of *Henry VI* and the play of which he is the eponymous hero, and it is fascinating to realise how early Shakespeare had made up his mind as to the precise character of the destructive forces which later are given their supreme expression in Iago and evoke Othello's terrible cry:

> But yet the pity of it, Iago! O Iago, the pity of it, Iago!
>
> *Othello*, IV, i, 206–7

Richard's very first line is written to overtop his elder brother's, and it is completely 'in character':

> *Margaret*: He [York] is arrested, but will not obey;
>   His sons, he says, shall give their words for him.
> *York*: Will you not, sons?
> *Edward*: Ay, noble father, if our words will serve.
> *Richard*: And if words will not, then our weapons shall.
>
> *2 Henry VI*, v, i, 136–40

In the following scene Richard is given a single combat and a soliloquy, and in this soliloquy the lines of his character are laid down. Richard and Somerset fight, and Somerset is killed.

> *Richard*: So, lie thou there;
>   For underneath an alehouse' paltry sign,
>   The Castle in St Albans, Somerset
>   Hath made the wizard famous in his death.
>   Sword, hold thy temper; heart, be wrathful still:
>   Priests pray for enemies, but princes kill.   v, ii, 66–71

His mordant wit, cynicism, courage, remorselessness and ability to bear malice long, are all there. More important still is his refusal to accept the metaphysical sanctions recognised by his own community: to him a blow is stronger than a plighted word, the wisdom of the seer folly and the teaching of the Church beneath contempt. His language sometimes expresses a gratuitous callousness:

> Sprawl'st thou? Take that to end thy agony;
>
> *3 Henry VI*, v, v, 39

and there is a bitter irony in his wooing of Anne as she weeps beside the bier of his latest victim, which is not always perceived when *Richard III* is acted in isolation. Says Richard:

> That hand, which for thy love, did kill thy love,
> Shall, for thy love, kill a far truer love;
>
> *Richard III*, i, ii, 190–1

but he has already expressed the value of the love he offers:

> And this word 'love', which greybeards call divine,
> Be resident in men like one another
> And not in me.
>
> *3 Henry VI*, v, vi, 81–3

He is conscious of the pattern which he breaks; as he takes into his arms the baby nephew he is soon to murder, he protests:

> And, that I love the tree from whence thou sprang'st
> Witness the loving kiss I give the fruit.
> [*Aside*] To say the truth, so Judas kiss'd his master,
> And cried 'all hail', when as he meant all harm.
>
> v, vii, 31–4

The central tenet of his creed is:

> I have no brother, I am like no brother...
> ...I am myself alone.   v, vi, 80–3

Macbeth is a more tragic figure than either Edmund or Richard because he realises more fully the sacredness of the bonds he is nevertheless determined to break.

> ...He's here in double trust;
> First, as I am his kinsman and his subject,
> Strong both against the deed.
>
> *Macbeth*, i, vii, 12–14

The first price paid for the breaking of the ties which unite a man to an ordered society is, very naturally, loneliness. Richard, who had once accepted this with such confident pride, learned some inkling of its actual horror before his death.

I shall despair. There is no creature loves me;
And if I die, no soul shall pity me.

Richard III, v, iii, 200–1

Edmund fights off the same horror by clinging to the self-confidence that comes from the satisfaction of his lust, as when he mutters: 'Yet Edmund was beloved.' But Macbeth found too late that he had unwittingly sacrificed love—the known and valued love between him and the wife who, through his own action, died alone and left him alone at last.

She should have died hereafter;
There would have been a time for such a word.

Macbeth, v, v, 17–18

...my way of life
Is fall'n into the sear, the yellow leaf;
And that which should accompany old age,
As honour, love, obedience, troops of friends,
I must not look to have.

v, iii, 22–6

Henry IV suffers a smaller measure of this same loneliness in his estrangement from his eldest son and, like the other two, pays the penalty of sleeplessness, though not of bad dreams. Out of many possible quotations perhaps the following are sufficient to show the likeness in this respect between the three men. His wife's words best describe Richard's nights:

For never yet one hour in his bed
Have I enjoy'd the golden dew of sleep,
But have been waked by his timorous dreams.

Richard III, iv, i, 83–5

Later, he himself admits the reason for them:

Give me another horse: bind up my wounds,
Have mercy, Jesu!—Soft! I did but dream.
O coward conscience, how dost thou afflict me!

v, iii, 177–9

Henry makes no such admission, but the sleeplessness he understands well.

O sleep, O gentle sleep,
Nature's soft nurse, how have I frighted thee,
That thou no more wilt weigh my eyelids down
And steep my senses in forgetfulness?

2 Henry IV, III, i, 5–8

Macbeth knew that he had murdered more than forgetfulness.

Sleep that knits up the ravell'd sleave of care,
The death of each day's life, sore labour's bath,
Balm of hurt minds, great nature's second course,
Chief nourisher in life's feast.   II, ii, 37–40

He had exchanged health, cleansing and nourishment for

... the affliction of these terrible dreams
That shake us nightly.   III, ii, 18–19

It is a shrewd touch that Edmund, the young man, still finding satisfaction in the flesh, apparently slept well.

Both Richard and Macbeth are finally lost because their isolation brings them into the sin of despair. Richard says:

... I am in
So far in blood that sin will pluck on sin:

Richard III, IV, ii, 64–5

and later:

All several sins, all used in each degree,
Throng to the bar, crying all, Guilty! guilty!
I shall despair.   v, iii, 198–200

Macbeth's words re-echo his:

I am in blood
Stepp'd in so far that, should I wade no more,
Returning were as tedious as go o'er.   III, iv, 136–8

And to him life becomes

... a tale
Told by an idiot, full of sound and fury,
Signifying nothing.   v, v, 26–8

Henry IV tries to protect himself by a kind of fatalism:

> ... Are these things then necessities?
> Then let us meet them like necessities.
>
> *2 Henry IV*, III, i, 92–3

In this despair repentance becomes impossible. Richard and Macbeth do not even attempt it, but Henry does, and the most illuminating comparison in his case therefore is one with Claudius. Claudius prays, like Henry, for forgiveness, and like him again he would make some restitution if he could. As Henry would prefer to pardon the rebels, so Claudius would like to win Hamlet's friendship—provided the price were not too high. But both men allow their hands to be forced, and Claudius' support of Laertes' treachery is a fair parallel with Henry's tacit acceptance of Prince John's unscrupulousness at Gaultree Forest. Henry's lip-service to his need for atonement through a crusade, when his real motive is the establishment of his dynasty, makes him almost as much a hypocrite as Richard when he uses his breviary and two bishops to bolster his attempt to win that same 'state'. Claudius eschews a false front of religion, and is, moreover, self-critical enough to recognise the inefficacy of his repentance, which Henry never does.

> ... Then I'll look up;
> My fault is past. But, O, what form of prayer
> Can serve my turn? 'Forgive me my foul murder'?
> That cannot be; since I am still possess'd
> Of those effects for which I did the murder,
> My crown, mine own ambition and my queen.
> May one be pardon'd and retain the offence?
> In the corrupted currents of this world
> Offence's gilded hand may shove by justice,
> ... but 'tis not so above;
> There is no shuffling, there the action lies
> In his true nature.
>
> *Hamlet*, III, iii, 50–63

When Henry IV prayed:

> How I came by the crown, O God forgive;
>
> *2 Henry IV*, IV, v, 219

he was making exactly the same petition as Claudius through whose

49

lips Shakespeare clearly states the cost of personal salvation: restitution as well as repentance. Mercy, at the price of not 'retaining
the offence', is offered both Claudius and Macbeth 'between the
stirrup and the ground', but neither grasps it. There is indeed
no sign in the dialogue that either of them is able to see the
opportunity; nevertheless, the plot clearly defines it as offered,
approached and then refused.

> *Queen*: The queen carouses to thy fortune, Hamlet...
> *King*:   Gertrude, do not drink.
> *Queen*: I will, my lord; I pray you, pardon me.
> *King* [*aside*]: It is the poison'd cup: it is too late.
>
> *Hamlet*, V, ii, 300–3

But it was not too late. Claudius could have dashed the cup from
her hand, as a few minutes later the dying Hamlet dashes it from
Horatio's. But such an act meant exposure and certain death. The
danger to the woman whom he loved, and who, in her fashion,
loved him, might well have spurred Claudius to an act which would
have saved himself as well as her, but he loved himself and his stolen
crown more than his wife. The moment of his choice—and it is no
more than a moment—is like the one in which Portia makes her
offer to Shylock of his last chance and is refused.

> *Portia*:   Be merciful,
> Take thrice thy money; bid me tear the bond.
> *Shylock*: When it is paid according to the tenour.
>
> *Merchant of Venice*, IV, i, 233–5

Macbeth also is given this final chance. It is in character that he
glimpses its importance, but no more than the others does he take
it. Macbeth no longer cares to keep the 'top of sovereignty', but
there is another barrier to repentance which is the hardest of all for
'fallen' man to overleap; the pride of Lucifer remains his even in
defeat:

> *Macduff*:   Turn, hell-hound, turn!
> *Macbeth*: Of all men else I have avoided thee:
> But get thee back; my soul is too much charged
> With blood of thine already....

> I'll not fight with thee.
> *Macduff*: Then yield thee, coward....
> *Macbeth*:   I will not yield,
> To kiss the ground before young Malcolm's feet,
> And to be baited with the rabble's curse.   v, viii, 3–29

In each case the price appears too high to be payable, but life offers the opportunity to pay it. After that, as at Doomsday, it is 'too late to seek abundance of thy grace'. Another parallel case exists; it is that of Henry V.

> More will I do;
> Though all that I can do is nothing worth,
> Since that my penitence comes after all,
> Imploring pardon.   IV, i, 319–22

Henry is the last man to consider making the one sacrifice that could bring his conscience peace: as firmly as Claudius did, he 'retains the offence'.

The Christian tradition of the rebel angel and the 'glozing' serpent, who by his cunning was successful in seducing Eve, has, in these plays, been conflated with the contemporary Renaissance 'machiavel'. Henry IV has here been identified with this dual figure, and this identity reinforces the interpretation of the whole of the second tetralogy as ultimately—though not always superficially—concerned with king-killing and usurpation, and can be used to illuminate that prime anomaly among Shakespearean heroes, Henry V.

2. TWO AMBIGUOUS FIGURES

Henry V and Octavius Caesar

At the centre of Shakespeare's portrait of the Elizabethans' hero king is the prayer before Agincourt:

> Not to-day, O Lord,
> O, not to-day, think not upon the fault
> My father made in compassing the crown!
> I Richard's body have interred new;

And on it have bestow'd more contrite tears
Than from it issued forced drops of blood:
...More will I do.

Henry V, IV, i, 309–19

These lines are of crucial importance; they are among the few given to Henry that sing and do not shout or orate or merely talk, and they occur at a critical moment, one of those points of rest, where into the stillness words drop with a maximum of significance. It is at such a moment and with such verse that Shakespeare reminds us that Henry's crown is stained with blood.

Having, for whatever reason, chosen to write a play about Henry V, for a London audience in about the year 1599, Shakespeare had no alternative but to write of a hero—valiant, modest and successful in war as in love. He apparently does so, recreating the contemporary historical myth with complete success. Yet the central figure is unaccountably difficult of assessment. This, it is suggested, is owing to a division in the author's mind. Shakespeare respected—and very possibly in a measure shared—the popular estimate of Henry. The country was living through a prolonged period of crisis; men were fighting and dying in France. Many modern critics who find the patriotism of the play chauvinistic today responded to it wholeheartedly in the atmosphere of 1945, appreciating Sir Laurence Olivier's film at the same level as the original audience appreciated the play. But the dissatisfaction, the nagging doubts, returned with calmer days, and it is difficult not to believe that Shakespeare shared them. To him Henry's place in the historical sequence was that of successor to the man who killed a king and one moreover who had repeatedly been presented as the direct and visible symbol of God himself.

Yet I well remember
The favours of these men: were they not mine?
Did they not sometime cry, 'all hail!' to me?
So Judas did to Christ:

Richard II, IV, i, 167–70

It is true that many such references are in Richard's own mouth, and in a realistic drama their value as evidence of the dramatist's intention would be weakened by Richard's own weaknesses, but in a poetic play the music and rhythm of the lines are decisive in determining an audience's response. The quality of the writing ensures that we are ready to remember the broken looking-glass and the shadow of a sorrow which destroyed the shadow of a face, even on the field of Agincourt, and the dramatist cannot have been unaware of this.

Henry V accepted his crown from his usurping father with his eyes open.

> *King Henry*:   God knows my son,
> By what by-paths and indirect crook'd ways
> I met this crown; and I myself know well
> How troublesome it sat upon my head.
> To thee it shall descend with better quiet, . . .
> For all the soil of the achievement goes
> With me into the earth. . . .

The Prince, however, does not hesitate—

> My gracious liege,
> You won it, wore it, kept it, gave it me;
> Then plain and right must my possession be.

The casuistry could not be better emphasised, and the next couplet implies that no price is thought too high:

> Which I with more than with a common pain
> 'Gainst all the world will rightfully maintain.
>   *2 Henry IV*, IV, v, 184–225

'You won it, wore it, kept it, gave it me.' It is significant that the harsh monosyllables awake in the memory echoes of a gentler voice, heard when, with unaccustomed cynicism, Richard watching the same impassive face as Hal did, remarked:

> they well deserve to have,
> That know the strong'st and surest way to get.
>   *Richard II*, III, iii, 200–1

This is the perfect statement of Henry IV's claim, a claim which exists in the realm of 'Realpolitik' and nowhere else. In other words, Hal knew what his inheritance was and accepted it in that knowledge. The *non sequitur* of 'Then plain and right must my possession be', serves only to emphasise the original jibe from Richard.

Hal claims the crown by descent but knows he must be prepared to defend it by force.

> Lo, here it sits,
> Which God shall guard; and put the world's whole strength
> Into one giant arm, it shall not force
> This lineal honour from me: this from thee
> Will I to mine leave as 'tis left to me.

2 Henry IV, IV, v, 43-7

'As 'tis left to me': that means doubtfully and only to be held by force ruthlessly applied. Henry's son proved an unsuitable recipient of such a sinister legacy. It is true but irrelevant that in this historical situation it is inconceivable that Henry should do other than accept and defend the crown, for a part of the present argument is that the very nature of the historical material is such as would inevitably produce such inconsistencies. These plays make two statements: the surface statement that Henry receives and defends what is his right, and below it—the clearer to read when the glitter of a public performance has faded—a second. This reports that Henry occupies, not by inheritance only but by conscious choice also, the throne of a murdered king. He 'repents', it is true, but Shakespeare shows through Claudius the petty value of such half-repentance and through Macbeth the emptiness of a stolen crown.

Henry V has many virtues which are of value in the body politic, but he 'retains the offence', and though during his reign stability is achieved, rebellion crushed in embryo and the nation united in a foreign war, yet the recovery is temporary, and the payment of the price of blood is only postponed. Apparently a very different man from his father, Hal shares with him one dominant characteristic: he deliberately chooses to emancipate himself from the bonds to which humanity should submit. Hal admits in words his bond to God, but like the other 'machiavels' he cultivates a deliberate 'non-attachment' to humanity, and Shakespeare reveals this both in his words and in his behaviour.

> I know you all, and will awhile uphold
> The unyoked humour of your idleness:
> Yet herein will I imitate the sun,
> Who doth permit the base contagious clouds
> To smother up his beauty from the world,
> That, when he please again to be himself,
> Being wanted, he may be more wonder'd at.
>
> *1 Henry IV*, I, ii, 219–25

This is the speech of a man who takes from others exactly what he wants—crown or companionship, love or amusement, the kingdom of England or the kingdom of France. He dismisses Falstaff, forgets Poins, executes Bardolph, sends Cambridge, Scroop and Grey to death, all with equal ease. Although one critic claims that he dismisses Scroop 'with a sob', and the verse certainly takes wing during this speech, the situation is essentially as remote from emotion as the more famous dismissal of Falstaff. It is not by coincidence that a special quality of music occurs in these lines, the content of which is quite at variance with the character of the speaker.

> What shall I say to thee, Lord Scroop?...
> Thou that didst bear the key of all my counsels,
> That knew'st the very bottom of my soul,
> That almost mightst have coin'd me into gold,
> Wouldst thou have practis'd on me for thy use,
> May it be possible, that foreign hire
> Could out of thee extract one spark of evil
> That might annoy my finger?
>
> *Henry V*, II, ii, 94–102

Henry was not a man with the right to condemn anyone for practising on another *for his use*; but Shakespeare could never stand completely detached from a story of 'man's ingratitude' and perhaps these lines give us a fleeting glimpse not of Henry's mind but of his creator's.

Henry's gaiety and ease of manner do not present any obstacles to identifying him with the more obvious 'machiavels'. On the contrary they are common elements in Shakespeare's picture of the type. It seems as though he felt that only by exceptional charm could such men hope to blind their fellows to their essentially predatory purposes. Even Falconbridge, from his ebullient first entry to his temporary adoption of a machiavellian allegiance to 'commodity', has not a more delightful buoyancy than Edmund. Richard III's animal spirits under the stimulus of danger are infectious.

> Stir with the lark to-morrow, gentle Norfolk...
> Come, bustle, bustle; caparison my horse.
> ...let us to't pell-mell.
>   V, iii, 55, 289, 312

Iago was apparently always popular; Desdemona herself enjoyed his company, and with his songs and his jokes he was as welcome to the gentle Cassio as to the foolish Roderigo. Even Macbeth is gifted with a winning graciousness, and it is only because actor and audience alike have such a plethora of riches to contend with that the fact is not always obvious in the theatre.

> Kind gentlemen, your pains
> Are register'd where every day I turn
> The leaf to read them,
>   I, iii, 150-2

he says, wringing the hands of Ross and Angus. And Duncan looks forward to visiting him with genuine pleasure:

> Let's after him,
> Whose care is gone before to bid us welcome:
> It is a peerless kinsman.
>   I, iv, 56-8

The graciousness that won those 'golden opinions' should be made clear in the opening scenes, for it is the same that he desperately strives to exercise after he is king, and which he knows deserts him. In Edmund, as in Falconbridge, this charm is closely related to a zest for life, as though the challenge of facing the universe untrammelled by scruples was intoxicatingly delightful. But if we have the slightest inclination to be fascinated by it, we need only remember Edmund leaving his father to the tender mercies of Cornwall, on the night of a storm which might well have shaken the complacency of the coolest heart.

How then, if by situation and character Henry V is clearly of the line of the 'machiavels', could Shakespeare adapt this child of his imagination to a play written to please an audience determined to admire and love their 'patriot king'? He succeeds in this apparently impossible task by creating a character which convincingly embodies the two apparently contradictory conceptions. In Henry V Shakespeare presents a man whose deliberately adopted machiavellian 'non-attachment' may fail him in a crisis, so that he becomes involved with humanity against his will and momentarily loses his defences. This quality of Hal's character, fully developed in the story of Agincourt, is indicated in 2 *Henry IV*, where his relationship with his father is given unexpected over-tones.

Prince: Shall I tell thee one thing, Poins?
Poins: Yes, faith, and let it be an excellent good thing....
Prince: Marry, I tell thee, it is not meet that I should be sad, now my father is sick: albeit I could tell to thee, as to one it pleases me, for fault of a better to call my friend, I could be sad, and sad indeed too.
Poins: Very hardly upon such a subject.
Prince: By this hand, thou thinkest me as far in the devil's book as thou and Falstaff.... But I tell thee, my heart bleeds inwardly that my father is so sick: and keeping such vile company as thou art hath in reason taken from me all ostentation of sorrow.   2 *Henry IV*, II, ii, 37–55

Very occasionally his creator allows a touch of sincere feeling to find expression amid the formal rhetoric which usually characterises dialogue between Henry IV and his eldest son. The passionate, repetitive rhythm of:

> Do not think so; you shall not find it so:
> 1 Henry IV, III, ii, 129

rings true, and so does the last half line of:

> God witness with me, when I here came in,
> And found no course of breath within your majesty,
> How cold it struck my heart!
> 2 Henry IV, IV, v, 150–2

But when we remember what Shakespeare sometimes makes of the relationship between parent and child there seems little enough warmth in this one.

The prince is shown, however, as genuinely stirred by his own accession to the crown. Shakespeare appears to have realised with peculiar intensity the crowding emotions which must sway a young monarch mounting his father's throne. They add a quivering sensibility to the modest words of Malcolm after the death of Macbeth, and he allows them to touch the usually cold heart of Henry Plantagenet, giving him an unwonted gentleness.

> This new and gorgeous garment, majesty,
> Sits not so easy on me as you think.
> Brothers, you mix your sadness with some fear;
> This is the English, not the Turkish court.
> Not Amurath an Amurath succeeds,
> But Harry Harry....
> I'll be your father and your brother too;
> Let me but bear your love, I'll bear your cares.
>
> *2 Henry IV*, v, ii, 44–58

Such tenderness stirs in him again on the night before Agincourt. In spite of the mordant jesting with Williams and Bates he was suddenly touched by the plight of the tiny army surrounded in the darkness by its enemies, by the pathos of his lonely, helpless soldiers, by his vision that the victory he hopes to win is not for himself alone but for them all, by his unexpected realisation of his responsibility for everyone there:

> The day, my friends and all things stay for me.
>
> *Henry V*, iv, i, 325

The words convey a humble, wondering acceptance of the role of leadership.

The same sudden, and to Henry himself surprising, involvement partially redeems the wooing of Katharine from the coarse, political bluster which it is sometimes said to be, and as which it certainly begins.

> To say to thee that I shall die, is true; but for thy love, by the Lord, no; *yet I love thee too*.[1]
>
> v, ii, 159–60

---

[1] Italics the author's.

One can feel the check, the pause, the change of rhythm which show the actor how he may capture the surprise with which the wooer realises the birth of a genuine emotion. The speech changes in quality, the excitement mounts, as his 'blood begins to flatter' him that he desires and is desired. There is real feeling as he takes her into his arms with the words: 'Therefore, patiently and yielding . . .' which prepares us for the wondering murmur after the silence of his kiss: 'You have witchcraft in your lips, Kate.' Only a few minutes later, however, he has escaped from his emotion and is driving his hard bargain and making his bawdy jokes with Burgundy and the king. Not an unusual change perhaps, but here it seems deeply characteristic of the man.

If Henry is indeed the individualist, the unscrupulous 'getter' whose allegiance to 'commodity' could nevertheless occasionally be pierced by an attack on his heart, the earlier scenes with Falstaff fall more easily into their place. We can understand that Shakespeare intended to show us Hal responding to Falstaff's wit and light-hearted iconoclasm—as the rhythm and vigour of the language insist that he did. Between those two the current leapt genuinely enough; for a time they were neither of them—as their very similar philosophies of life dictated—simply self-sufficient and self-seeking. But Henry, free of two worlds for a while, soon made his choice and had re-established his independence of his friend long before he publicly rejected him. The most highly charged scene between Hal and Falstaff is the first, and even here the emotional warmth springs from Falstaff, not from the prince. It may be only a coincidence that we hear Shakespeare at work with the magic he elicits from the use of a repeated Christian name. Coriolanus and Othello are both given this trick of speech when they appeal in desperate loneliness to a false friend, and so it is not without interest that Falstaff uses it with Hal, on an occasion apparently so different and so cheerful.

Thou hast done much harm upon me, Hal; God forgive thee for it! Before I knew thee, Hal, I knew nothing; and now am I, if a man should speak truly, little better than one of the wicked....Why, Hal,

59

'tis my vocation, Hal; 'tis no sin for a man to labour in his vocation.[1]

1 Henry IV, I, ii, 102–17

This is tender chaffing indeed, and Hal must be relishing it and responding at least in part, but his own tone is very different:

Prince: A purse of gold most resolutely snatched on Monday night and most dissolutely spent on Tuesday morning; got with swearing 'Lay by' and spent with crying 'Bring in'; now in as low an ebb as the foot of the ladder and by and by in as high a flow as the ridge of the gallows....

Falstaff: I prithee, sweet wag, shall there be gallows standing in England when thou art king?... Do not thou, when thou art king, hang a thief.

Prince: No; thou shalt.

Falstaff: Shall I? O rare! By the Lord, I'll be a brave judge.

Prince: Thou judgest false already: I mean, thou shalt have the hanging of the thieves and so become a rare hangman.

Falstaff: Well, Hal, well.

I, ii, 39–77

Falstaff bears no malice for the snub, but the greater refusal to come gives poignancy to the naively eager speech-rhythms of his question and exclamation. In the episode of 'excellent sport' when first Falstaff and then the prince play the part of the king, there can be no doubt whose fooling is the more gracious. The prince's language has a flavour almost nauseous, which indicates that any feeling he once had for Falstaff has been cast away.

Prince: ...there is a devil haunts thee in the likeness of an old fat man; ...Why dost thou converse with that trunk of humours, that bolting-hutch of beastliness, that swollen parcel of dropsies, that huge bombard of sack, that stuffed cloak-bag of guts, that roasted Manningtree ox with the pudding in his belly....

Falstaff: I would your grace would take me with you: whom means your grace?... for sweet Jack Falstaff, kind Jack Falstaff... and therefore more valiant, being, as he is, old Jack Falstaff, banish not him thy Harry's company: banish plump Jack, and banish all the world.

Prince: I do, I will.

II, iv, 492–528

---

[1] But yet the pity of it, Iago! O Iago, the pity of it, Iago!

Othello, IV, I, 206–7

Aufidius, though I cannot make true wars,
I'll frame convenient peace. Now, good Aufidius,
Were you in my stead, would you have heard
A mother less? or granted less, Aufidius? *Coriolanus*, V, iii, 190–3

Again the warning sounds, but the act which it appears to foretell has in reality already taken place. One feels inclined—Brabantio-wise—to agree with Falstaff when he complains that he must have 'taken medicines' to make him love this cold-blooded young man, particularly when one realises that at the very moment he makes this protest he believes that the prince has hidden his horse. The play-acting scene is the last intimate meeting between Falstaff and the Prince, for at their later encounter at Mistress Quickly's Falstaff's attention is elsewhere, and he has in fact just given his shrewdest summing-up of the prince's character:

A good shallow young fellow: a' would have made a good pantler, a' would ha' chipped bread well.   *2 Henry IV*, II, iv, 257–8

There is no more talk of love philtres.

Falstaff's own attitude is of course a genuine and brilliant example of ambivalence. His conscious philosophy of life is as machiavellian as Hal's own, and his marauding expeditions to Gloucestershire show him as ruthless as ever his prince could be:

if the young dace be a bait for the old pike, I see no reason in the law of nature but I may snap at him.   III, ii, 355–7

His allegiance is divided between the values of two distinct worlds. When news of Hal's accession reaches him his first reaction is utterly unscrupulous, though generous as well.

Away, Bardolph! saddle my horse. Master Robert Shallow, choose what office thou wilt in the land, 'tis thine. Pistol, I will double-charge thee with dignities.... Let us take any man's horses; the laws of England are at my commandment.   V, iii, 127–32

It is easy to dismiss the excitement while he waits for the newly crowned king as selfish and the emotion of his greeting as merely histrionic, but the situation is not so simple. If it were, what is to account for the death scene in *Henry V*, and his followers' poignant explanation of it?

Nym: The king hath run bad humours on the knight; that's the even of it.

Pistol: Nym, thou hast spoke the right;
His heart is fracted and corroborate.
                                    Henry V, II, i, 127-30

Shakespeare has elsewhere written of a parallel situation in which a young friend, admired although criticised, betrays the love of an older man. There are certain lines in some of the sonnets between nos. 87 and 112 which are curiously relevant to his portrait of Henry. The lines

> That tongue that tells the story of thy days,
> Making lascivious comments on thy sport,
> Cannot dispraise but in a kind of praise;
> Naming thy name blesses an ill report,
>   Sonnet 95, 5-8

strongly suggest the ambivalent attitude to the royal hero which breaks the play apart. So does

> Thou makest faults graces that to thee resort.
> As on the finger of a throned queen
> The basest jewel will be well esteem'd,
> So are those errors that in thee are seen.   Sonnet 96, 4-7

The best comment on the scene in which Falstaff is disowned is found in the famous lines concerning the men

> Who, moving others, are themselves as stone,
> Unmoved, cold, and to temptation slow.
> They rightly do inherit heaven's graces
> And husband nature's riches from expense;
> They are the lords and owners of their faces,
> Others but stewards of their excellence.
>   Sonnet 94, 3-8

'Stone' and 'cold' have pejorative overtones which are reinforced by their uses elsewhere in Shakespeare's work,[1] and it is equally true that the possible parallels with Falstaff are all sympathetic ones.
The friend who is in the time of life

> When yellow leaves, or none, or few, do hang
> Upon those boughs which shake against the cold,
>   Sonnet 73, 2-3

---

[1] E.g. Toad, that under cold stone
Days and nights has thirty-one. *Macbeth*, IV, i, 6-7

pleads that for his conduct Fortune should be blamed:

> The guilty goddess of my harmful deeds,
> That did not better for my life provide
> Than public means which public manners breeds.
>
> Sonnet III, 2–4

He too hopes his friendship may be preserved if he is content to hide it:

> I will acquaintance strangle and look strange,
> Be absent from thy walks,[1] and in my tongue
> Thy sweet beloved name[2] no more shall dwell.
>
> Sonnet 89, 8–10

Finally, the poet foresees for himself the death which he allotted to Falstaff:

> But do thy worst to steal thyself away,
> For term of life thou art assured mine,
> And life no longer than thy love will stay,
> For it depends upon that love of thine.   Sonnet 92, 1–4

The truth appears on the lips of simple men:

> The king hath run bad humours on the knight...
> Nym, thou hast spoke the right.

Whatever his historical material made necessary in the plotting of his play, the poems make plain where, according to Shakespeare, the true values lay. When the king's voice cuts the air with the words 'I know thee not, old man,' all the glittering panoply of the coronation procession is torn aside for a moment to show the abyss where human beings betray each other's trust and where a young man may break an old man's heart. The love so deliberately rejected was real, and it is the manner of Falstaff's death which proves it. There had been a warning: 'Banish plump Jack and banish all the world.' 'I do. I will.' The world which Hal banished with such easy assurance contained more than he knew.

The interpretation of Henry as a man deeply divided within himself is reinforced by a consideration of the abnormally violent and

---

[1] Cf. I shall be sent for soon at night.   [2] *Henry IV*, v. v, 94.   [2] Cf. above, p. 59.

unpleasant emotionalism of some of the young king's speeches on war, which is stressed by Mr Traversi in his recent book.[1] He notices particularly the speech before Harfleur and remarks on its gratuitous threats of sexual outrage:

> If I begin the battery once again,
> I will not leave the half-achieved Harfleur
> Till in her ashes she lie buried.
> The gates of mercy shall be all shut up,
> And the flesh'd soldier, rough and hard of heart,
> In liberty of bloody hand shall range
> With conscience wide as hell, mowing like grass
> Your fresh-fair virgins and your flowering infants.
> What is it then to me, if impious war,
> Array'd in flames like to the prince of fiends,
> Do, with his smirched complexion, all fell feats
> Enlink'd to waste and desolation?
> What is't to me, when you yourselves are cause,
> If your pure maidens fall into the hand
> Of hot and forcing violation?
> What rein can hold licentious wickedness
> When down the hill he holds his fierce career?
>
> *Henry V*, III, iii, 7–23

All this is horrible and Shakespeare of course knew it to be so. The nature of his own response to physical violence is proved by the trembling awareness shown in much of his animal imagery:

> And as the butcher bears away the calf
> And binds the wretch and beats it when it strays,
> Bearing it to the bloody slaughter-house,
> Even so remorseless have they borne him hence;
> And as the dam runs lowing up and down,
> Looking the way her harmless young one went,
> And can do nought but wail her darling's loss,
> Even so myself bewails good Gloucester's case.
>
> *2 Henry VI*, III, i, 210–17

'The hot scent-snuffing hounds', though the musician in Shake-

[1] *Shakespeare's History Plays*, 1958.

speare could enjoy the sound of their baying, particularly 'in the distant valley', could not swing his sympathy from hunted to hunter:

> By this, poor Wat, far off upon a hill,
> Stands on his hinder legs with listening ear,
> To hearken if his foes pursue him still:...
> Then shalt thou see the dew-bedabbled wretch
> Turn and return, indenting with the way;
> Each envious brier his weary legs doth scratch,
> Each shadow makes him stop, each murmur stay.
>
> *Venus and Adonis*, ll. 697–708

Since the dumb victims of man's violence present themselves to his mind in these colours it is impossible that Shakespeare wrote such words as Henry's without being aware of their implications.

The only man who rivals Henry in the violence of his language about the ravages of war is Timon, who in the desperation of his misanthropy urges Alcibiades to ravish Athens in words hardly stronger than Henry's own.

> *Timon*: If Alcibiades kill my countrymen,
> Let Alcibiades know this of Timon,
> That Timon cares not. But if he sack fair Athens,
> And take our goodly aged men by the beards,
> Giving our holy virgins to the stain
> Of contumelious, beastly, mad-brain'd war,
> Then let him know, and tell him Timon speaks it,
> In pity of our aged and our youth,
> I cannot choose but tell him, that I care not.
>
> *Timon of Athens*, v, i, 172–80

The parallel is sufficiently startling to suggest that Shakespeare thought things about his hero king that could not be openly proclaimed in the play of his victories but which could be insinuated so as to make the judicious grieve. Moreover it is certain that such hysterical over-emphasis and obsession with the horrors of what he was doing would be a likely element of a guilt-ridden and divided mind. Mr Traversi also points out Henry's habit of endeavouring to put the responsibility of his own acts of violence on to others, as he does at Harfleur and also before declaring war on France—another realistic touch in the portrait of a neurotic who has deliberately suppressed his more honest and generous qualities but has by no means inhibited them entirely.

Beside Henry V it is illuminating to place for a moment the figure of another successful politician, Octavius Caesar, for his place in history was, like Henry's, a peculiarly honourable one, to the Elizabethan imagination. Not only was his name associated with the greatest era of Latin literature, but he had brought to the world the age of peace in which the Christ was born. This conception influences his presentation by Shakespeare; his power is equal to his own famous lines:

> But let determined things to destiny
> Hold unbewail'd their way.
>
> *Antony and Cleopatra*, III, vi, 83-4

Moreover, the issue of the struggle with Antony is admittedly one on which the fortune of the world depends.

> The time of universal peace is near:
> Prove this a prosperous day, the three-nook'd world
> Shall bear the olive freely.   IV, vi, 4-6

But as a person Octavius is even more inadequate to his historical role than was Henry Plantagenet. He shares the English king's basic 'machiavellian' heresy that personal righteousness is irrelevant to affairs of state, and he succeeds in identifying himself so completely with Rome that he believes Antony is to be condemned principally because in all his 'lascivious wassails' he 'hardly . . . vouchsafed to think he had partners'. Later he insists that Antony must

> No way excuse his soils, when *we*[1] do bear
> So great weight in his lightness.   I, iv, 24-5

Personal loyalty means nothing to him. Although he admits his obligations to Lepidus with the significant words

> I knew it for my bond: I, iv, 84

he liquidates the 'slight unmeritable man' as soon as he safely can,

[1] Italics the author's.

albeit the charge of cruelty comes strangely from one as ruthless as himself against his anxious and over-diplomatic partner. He genuinely expects Cleopatra to be willing to buy safety by betraying Antony.

> The queen
> Of audience nor desire shall fail, so she
> From Egypt drive her all-disgraced friend,
> Or take his life there.   III, xii, 20-3

The casual contempt in the last five words makes them a revealing touch of characterisation. He himself gives the sister whom he apparently loves with sincerity to a man whom he both despises and mistrusts, in order to win a political advantage, and his pledged word is merely the small change of diplomacy. To Cleopatra's messenger he says:

> She soon shall know of us, by some of ours,
> How honourable and how kindly we
> Determine for her; for Caesar cannot live
> To be ungentle.   v, i, 57-60

To his own envoy, however, his words are:

> Go and say,
> We purpose her no shame: give her what comforts
> The quality of her passion shall require,
> Lest, in her greatness, by some mortal stroke
> She do defeat us; for her life in Rome
> Would be eternal in our triumph: v, i, 61-6

This is the man whom Cleopatra finally defeats.

Cleopatra's love was certainly very different from Juliet's or Cordelia's, and she drew Mark Antony into a perilous country in which he destroyed himself as well as her, but the world from which he was lured by his 'serpent of old Nile' was neither innocent nor gracious. It was the world of the hard bargain and the proscription list, the loveless world of the 'machiavel', from which it was surely good for him to escape, although he was judged by his peers to have failed so calamitously in that Egypt where he became 'passion's slave', 'a pipe for Fortune's finger to sound what stop she please'.

It is very possible that Shakespeare may have thought that machiavellism was a necessity for every successful ruler; Volumnia urges it upon her son with great persuasiveness.

> I have heard you say,
> Honour and policy, like unsever'd friends,
> I' the war do grow together:...
> If it be honour in your wars to seem
> The same you are not, which, for your best ends,
> You adopt your policy, how is it less or worse,
> That it shall hold companionship in peace
> With honour, as in war,...
> ...it lies you on to speak
> To the people; not by your own instruction,
> Nor by the matter which your heart prompts you,
> But with such words that are but roted in
> Your tongue,...
> Now, this no more dishonours you at all
> Than to take in a town with gentle words,
> Which else would put you to your fortune and
> The hazard of much blood.
>
> *Coriolanus*, III, ii, 41–61

This advice, which would sound well on the lips of Henry V or Octavius Caesar, Coriolanus appears to take but fails to put into practice. He causes great suffering, and he dies miserably. As a ruler he is a complete failure. Nevertheless, both his life and his death call forth from his creator a music and a sympathy that never grace the lives of his more successful predecessors.

PART II

TWO DAUGHTERS OF GOD:
THE CONFLICT BETWEEN JUSTICE
AND MERCY

CHAPTER III

THE PARLIAMENT OF HEAVEN

1. SOME PRE-SHAKESPEAREAN STATEMENTS

Under the Luciferian sin Shakespeare subsumes man's many acts of rebellion against his God. Once the validity of an absolute command has been admitted and the command broken, an obsessional sense of guilt becomes inevitable. Hence the persistent concern of medieval art and literature with the judgment of God in its double aspect of the justice deserved and the mercy so urgently needed. This concern can be well illustrated by the popularity of the debate between the four virtues who came to be known as the Daughters of God. They are named in Psalm lxxxv, verse 10, 'Mercy and Truth are met together; Righteousness[1] and Peace have kissed each other.' The tradition of dramatising the conflict between Justice and Mercy as a debate or trial is very ancient, going back at least to the action between the Erinyes and Apollo for the life of Orestes in the *Oresteia*, and the use of legal imagery by Shakespeare in this connection is one of the clearest examples of the influence of medieval patterns on his imagination.

The symbol of a debate between the Daughters concerning the fate of mankind spread rapidly over Europe where it appears in the literatures of France, Italy, Provence, Germany, Holland, Hungary and Spain as well as of England. It occurs first in the eleventh century in a version of the rabbinical Midrash. The first important Christian application of the allegory is made by St Bernard of Clairvaux (1091-1153) in a sermon, *In Festo Annunciationis Beatae Virginis*, and the earliest known English mention of the Daughters is in the dialogue *Vices and Virtues* (c. 1200).[2] In this early version, unlike those which followed, the balance between the Daughters is not held evenly, for Truth maintains that God is himself on Mercy's

---

[1] Righteousness or Justice. [2] Early English Text Society: Original Series, LXXXIX.

side. The personification is somewhat confused, as Truth speaks both as one of the four Daughters and also, apparently, as the Son of God, but the position is of interest since it is the one to which Shakespeare finally returned.

Then said Truth: 'That is right that God's mercy, is ever higher and more than His right-judgment.'

The material appears more fully developed in *Cursor Mundi* (c. 1325)[1] as the story of a king, his son, his daughters and an imprisoned 'thrall', and is fully elaborated by John Lydgate in his *Life of Our Lady*, Book II (c. 1420).[2]

> The first of all cruelly to threte
> Trouthe began almost in a rage
> Of cruel ire and of melencolye
> And seide shortly that man for his outrage
> Of verre right must nedys die
> And thus began the controversie.

The resolution of the controversy here so ominously begun comes only with the promise of the Incarnation.

> And there shall Peace kiss Rightwiseness
> And all the sisters accord in that place,
> And Right shall leave all her sturdyness
> And Truth's sword shall no more menace
> And finally Mercy shall purchase
> A charter of pardon....
> When the lion maketh his habitacle
> Within a maid but of tender age.   Stanza 177

Langland treats the allegory in his own individual way:[3]

> Then I withdrew into that darkness and descended into hell.
> And there I saw coming, according to the Scripture,
> A young woman, walking out of a western region,
> And as she went her ways, her eyes were watching hell.
> Mercy was that maiden's name, a meek thing she was,
> Benign as a bride, obedient in her speech.

[1] Early English Text Society: Original Series, LIX.
[2] Edited by S. Quintin in unpublished thesis for the University of London.
[3] *Visions from Piers Plowman*, translated into modern English by N. Coghill (1949).

After Christ's triumph over 'your lying Lucifer, that laid a snare for Eve', Truth and Righteousness both admit the triumph of his love and turn to Peace.

> 'Truce!' said Truth, 'You tell truly, by Jesus!
> Close with me in covenant, and let us kiss the other!'
> 'And let no people,' said Peace, 'perceive that we wrangled!
> For nothing is impossible to God Almighty.'...
> Till the day dawned these damsels were dancing,
> So that men rang out the Resurrection; and right with
> that I woke.

Meanwhile, Cardinal Bonaventura of Padua had written the *Meditationes Vitae Christi* which determined the form of the first English dramatic version of this material. He sets his action in heaven and precedes the debate of the Daughters by prayers for man offered by the angelic hosts before the throne of God; his work was translated into English by Nicholas Love in 1410.[1]

In the *Ludus Coventriae* there is placed between the material of the Old and New Testaments a play called *The Parliament of Heaven*. It opens with the angelic hosts pleading to God for Man's Salvation.

> *Virtutes*: Lord pleaseth it thy high domination
> On man that thou made to have pity:....
> For man to thine high majesty
> Mercy, mercy, mercy we cry.   ll. 35 ff.

The Four Daughters enter, and Truth restates the central dilemma:

> Lord I am thy daughter Truth,
> Thou wilt see I be not lore.
> Thine unkind creatures to save were ruth,
> The offence of man hath grieved thee sore.   ll. 57 ff.

Mercy pleads for man:

> O Father of mercy and god of comfort...
> Let your daughter Mercy to you resort
> And on man that is mischieved have compassion... ll. 73 ff.

---

[1] A full account of the many European versions of the allegory will be found in *The Four Daughters of God*, by Hope Traver, Bryn Mawr Monographs, vol. VI, to which the author is indebted for several of the facts in the preceding paragraphs.

Justice however stands with Truth:

> Man offended him that is endless
> Therefore his endless punishment may never cease
> Also he forsook his maker, that made him of clay
> And the devil to his master he chose,
> Should he be saved? Nay, nay, nay.
> As wise as God he would have been
> This was the abominable presumption.   ll. 92 ff.

Mercy answers:

> Sister Rightwiseness you are too vengeable...
> Ye must consider the frailness of mankind ...   ll. 105-10

It is Peace who persuades the disputants to submit their difference to the wisdom of God, and God the Son then speaks:

> If Adam had not died, perished had right-wiseness...
> If another death come not, Mercy should perish,
> Then Peace were exiled finally;
> So two deaths must be, you four to cherish.   ll. 139 ff.

He finally offers to pay himself the death penalty demanded by Justice:

> ... Since in my wisdom he began
> I am ready to do this deed.   ll. 179-80

The reconciliation of the opposites is thus achieved.

> *Misericordia*: Now is the loveday made of us four finally,
> Now may we live in peace as we were wont.
> Misericordia et Veritas obviaverunt sibi
> Justicia et Pax osculate sunt.
> et hic osculabunt pariter omnes.   ll. 185 ff.

The Castle of Perseverance,[1] dated by A. W. Pollard as mid-fifteenth century, uses the same debate for its final scene and in it makes dramatic use of symbolic costumes:

the four daughters shall be clad in mantles, Mercy in white, Rightwiseness in red altogether, Truth in sad green and Peace all in black.

                                              Before l. 1

---

[1] E.E.T.S. Extra Series 91. Spelling and punctuation modernised by the author.

The sisters' debate before God—'Pater, sedens in trono'—for the soul of Humanum Genus after his death on earth; the situation has thus become more individualised and dramatically urgent; Justice's blood-coloured mantle suggests legal robes and must have served well to enforce her caustic comment:

> As he has brewed, let him drink,
> The devil shall quit him his mead.　　　　ll. 3763–4

But God, after taking time to consider his verdict, bids his daughters fetch Humanum Genus, whom he freely pardons.

Although these are the only formal disputes between the Four Daughters in the English medieval drama[1] the case was very different on the Continent. The great French cycles were mostly written in their present form during the fourteenth and fifteenth centuries, and probably the most elaborate and beautiful of all the dramatic treatments of the theme is that to be found in the anonymous *Mistere du Viel Testament*.[2] Only two of the Daughters take part in the *Mistere*—Justice and Mercy—and their arguments before God form interludes which may occur at the beginning or in the middle of the plays. They first appear after the fall of Adam and Eve. The debate is formal and suggests the pleading in a court of law. Justice develops the case against Adam under formal headings and demands the death penalty:

> Sire Dieu, gardez vostre loy
> Et vous monstrez chef de justice.　　　　ll. 1459–60

Misericorde pleads the strength of the temptation which Adam had to face and the reality of his repentance:

> Sire, Dieu, soyez pitoyable
> Pour ceste douloureuse pomme.　　　　ll. 1465–6

Even in the case of Cain Mercy pleads for forgiveness:

> Se Cayn a esté deceu
> Et que le Dyable l'ayt tenté.　　　　ll. 2372–3

---

[1] At least in those plays which remain to us. It must be remembered that it is the more theological plays which are most likely to have disappeared at the destruction of the monasteries.

[2] Société des anciens Textes français, 1878, ed. by James de Rothschild.

But the blood of Abel cries for justice from the ground:

> *La Voix du Sang qui crie a Dieu*:
> Justice, Justice divine
> Venez le sang juste venger,
> Que voyez ainsi le danger!
> Abel est mort, mys a ruyne.
> *Justice*: Il est force que je m'encline
> A escouter ce messager.
> *La Voix*: Justice, Justice divine,
> Venez le sang juste venger!...   ll. 2752 ff.

The debate recurs regularly, and during the story of Abraham and Isaac, which itself prefigures the price of man's forgiveness, the heavenly voices are heard at the very climax of the play when Isaac is already bound on the altar.

> *Abram*: A Dieu, mon filz.
> *Isaac*:   A Dieu, mon pére.
> Recommandés moy a ma mere;
> Jamais je ne la reverray.
> *Abram*: A Dieu, mon filz.
> *Isaac*: A Dieu, mon pére.
> *Il luy bende les yeulx.*
> *Misericorde*: O Dieu tout puissant et parfaict,
> Regardés d'Abraham le faict....
> *Dieu*: Je changeray le sacrifice.
> Le povre enfant point ne mourra.   ll.10275-310

In *Le Mystère de la Passion* by A. Greban,[1] written perhaps half a century later, the tone has changed considerably, and the debate before God has become more drily legalistic in manner.

> *Justice*: jamais ne me consentiroye
> jusqu'a ce que le droit aroye
> que je me sentoye estre deu,
> et que de mon droit et mon deu
> je seroye satisfiée.

Among the disputants there appears the figure of Wisdom who is

---

[1] Ed. by Gaston Paris and Gaston Raynaud (Paris, 1878). MS. dated 1473.

called upon by God the Father to arbitrate between Justice and Mercy concerning the fate of Mankind. Miss Hope Traver[1] suggests that Sapience plays a role significantly similar to that of Portia standing between Antonio and Shylock; it is tempting to wonder if an English play using this pattern did once exist, but no example remains.

Mankind,[2] a play of about the same date as *The Castle of Perseverance*, develops similar material in another way. Mercy is here a priest, and he is opposed not on a philosophical plane to Justice but on a practical one to Mischief and his allies. These persuade Mankind that he can never receive mercy and so lead him into the deadly sin of Despair. In this state of mind he attempts to commit suicide, encouraged and instructed by his tormentors.

> *Mankind*: A rope! a rope! a rope! I am not worthy.
> *Mischief*: Anon, anon, anon! I have it here ready;
> With a tree also that I have got.
> Hold the tree, Now-a-days! Nought! take heed and be wise.

Mankind falls silent to the ground and his friends in macabre horseplay demonstrate the method of death they are advising upon New Guise, whom they have nearly succeeded in strangling in good earnest before they are interrupted by the entry of Mercy.

> *Mischief*: Help thyself, Nought! lo Mercy is here!
> He scareth us with a bales; we may no longer tarry.
> *New Guise*: Queek, queek, queek! alas, my throat! I beshrew
> you, marry!
> A, Mercy! Christ's copped curse go with you, and saint Davy.
> Alas, my weasand! ye were somewhat too near!

The play *Respublica* (1553)[3]—possibly by N. Udall—is of interest since it shows the persistence of this subject-matter into the drama of Queen Mary's reign and its secular development. The dispute between the Daughters has changed its setting, and their arguments have now become sociological rather than religious. The greater portion of the play is a lively attack on the economic evils let loose

---

[1] See above, p. 73, note 1.
[2] *Early English Dramatists*. 'Lost' Tudor Plays, ed. by J. S. Farmer (1907).   [3] *Ibid.*

on England by, in the writer's opinion, the Reformation. Respublica is helpless because she is deceived by evil councillors, Adulation, Insolence, Avarice and Oppression (who calls himself Reformation). The first four acts are extremely lively and well written, but when the 'good' characters arrive in Act v the dramatic interest falls away somewhat. Misericordia, or Lady Compassion, appears; she fetches Lady Verity—'Old Time's daughter' —and they are joined by Peace and Justice. Their conventional debate is fortunately enlivened by the 'bad' characters who are nervously awaiting its conclusion.

> *Justice*: Come on, Respublica! with us to wealth from woe:
>   God has given us in charge that it must be so.
> *Avarice*: [*Aside*] Have they kissed together?
> *Adulation*: [*Aside*] Yea!
> *Avarice*: [*Aside*] What needeth that?
>   Men should kiss women—and what point are they at?
> *Adulation*: [*Aside*] All the four sisters, I do you t'understand,
>   Have already taken Respublica in hand.

Justice brings forward the usual pragmatic arguments in support of the necessity for retribution.

> *Justice*: But how shall this redress be well persecuted,
>   If justice with mercy shall be executed?
>   Straight Justice must such great enormities redress;
>   Severity must put man in fear to transgress:
> *Misericordia*: If offenders were not, wherefore might mercy serve?
> *Adulation*: Stick hard to it, good, sweet Lady Compassion!
>   How we are all else undone, by Cock's bitter passion!
> *Misericordia*: Verity! how say you? have I not spoken well?
> *Verity*: Mercy in one place with Justice sometime may dwell,
>   And right well agree together—how say you Peace?   v, 10

Nemesis, the judge on this occasion, establishes a working compromise; she sentences Avarice to make 'full restitution', allowing People to 'squeeze him' as hard as he likes; Adulation is given a second chance, but the others fare worse:

> Because the fault of Insolence is heinous and great
>   Lucifer's own fault to aspire to the highest seat,   v, 10

he and the ringleader, Oppression—or Reformation—are sentenced to imprisonment.

The debates, although intellectually the clearest, are not the most moving examples of the juxtapositions of Justice and Mercy in the medieval theatre. These occur in the Doomsday plays which give such impressive endings to all the four miracle cycles. In them the long lines of saved souls either climb upward to the raised stage of Heaven or pass through its open gates, while the damned are driven by tormenting devils through the gaping mouth of Hell. The dialogue of this scene of final judgment is always based on the passage in St Matthew's gospel[1] in which the Son questions the souls about the 'deeds of mercy' they have performed during their lives, and the terrible urgency of the scene depends on the knowledge:

> 'Tis late to seek abundance of thy grace
> *When we are there ...*[2]

In the *Ludus Coventriae* we read:

> *The good spirits*: Ah mercy Lord for our misdeed
> And let thy mercy spring and spread.
> But alas we bide in dread
> It is too late to ask mercy.   *Doomsday*, ll. 36 ff.

God, however, declares that his dear children are burnished as 'bright as beryl' by his blessing, and they humbly enter the gates opened by Peter. When the damned souls, left outside, cry for mercy God replies:

> How would ye wretches any mercy have?
> To whom have ye done any merciful deed
> Mercy for to win?
> To hungry and thirsty that asked in my name
> Meat and drink would ye give none;
> Of naked men ye had no shame,
> Ye would not visit men in no prison.
> Ye had no pity on sick nor lame
> Deed of mercy would ye never done.   ll. 70–83

[1] Chapter xxv, vv. 34 ff.   [2] John Donne, *Holy Sonnets*. Italics the author's.

> *Omnes damnandi*: Ah mercy lord, mickle of might
> We ask thy mercy and not thy right.[1]   ll. 127–8 ff.

But for them it is too late.

The tradition of concluding a play with a formal and final judgment scene was carried forward into secular drama by the morality plays. The last scene in *The Castle of Perseverance* is the one already noticed in which the four Daughters of God appear. It is also a Judgment scene. The Daughters 'tunc ascendent ad Patrem omnes', that is, they go up on to God's scaffold for the formal trial of Mankind's soul. Again the note of 'too late' is sounded, and here it is enforced by the rhythm of the *Dies Irae*.

> *Justice*: Over late he called confession;
> Over light was his contrition;
> He made never satisfaction.   ll. 3428 ff.

But as we have seen, Mankind is forgiven. The Daughters are sent to lead him by the hand and all together 'tunc ascendant ad tronum'. The miracle tradition of the actual ascent of the saved souls to Heaven is thus repeated, and so also is the wording of the final judgment:

> *Pater* (*sedens in judicio*): The good on the right side
> shall stand full sure,
> The bad on the left side there shall I set.
> The seven deeds of mercy whoso hath used
> To fulfil—the hungry for to give meat,
> Or drink to the thirsty; to the naked vesture,
> The poor or the pilgrim home for to fetch,
> Or thy neighbour that hath need;
> Whoso doth mercy to his might
> To the sick or them in prison pyt,
> He doth to me: I shall him quit,
> Heaven's bliss shall be his meed....
> And they that evil do, they shall to Hell lake
> In bitter balys to be burnt: my judgment it is.   ll. 3627 ff.

Even Sir David Lindsay's fully secularised morality of the Three

---

[1] I.e. thy justice.

Estates[1] ends with a Judgment scene in which John is given

> a new habiliment
> Of satin damask or of velvet fine

and mounts to a seat aloft, while (instead of Hell's Mouth) a gallows is erected on the stage to ensure the punishment of the wicked.

A memory of the souls rising from their tombs in Doomsday plays or meeting their Redeemer in *The Harrowing of Hell* would explain the metaphor that Juliet used when she thought of her lover coming to rescue her from the similitude of death:

> How if, when I am laid into the tomb,
> I wake before the time that Romeo
> Come to redeem me? IV, iii, 30–2

It is even more likely that the tradition of finishing a man's story only with his final judgment is reflected in Othello's tragic cry:

> ... when we shall meet at compt,
> This look of thine will hurl my soul from heaven,
> And fiends will snatch at it. V, ii, 273–5

If this is an echo in the poet's mind of a traditional theme, this particular resonance appears to have become at last unbearable to him. *Othello* is in many ways a bridge between the tragedies and the romances, and it is of fundamental importance to a true interpretation of the last plays to realise that in them a Judgment involving a final condemnation does not appear.[2]

It was from the Christian tradition, however, that Shakespeare learned not only of the Judgment, but also of the Judge who returned in glory to pronounce it. In the York Doomsday play the Son proclaims his mission thus:

> And I am come as crowned king...
> My Father in heaven has me sent
> To deem your days and make ending.
> Come is the day of Judgement.

The royal deliverer who returns to his own people is a figure present in Shakespeare's mind from the beginning, and his treatment

---

[1] *Satire of the Three Estates*, ed. by T. Guthrie (Heinemann). [2] See p. 137.

of it will be considered later. Here it might be sufficient to think for a moment of Malcolm at the end of *Macbeth*.

> *Macduff*: Hail, King! for so thou art: behold, where stands
> The usurper's cursed head: the time is free:
> I see thee compass'd with thy kingdom's pearl,
> That speak my salutation in their minds,
> Whose voices I desire aloud with mine:
> Hail, King of Scotland!...
> *Malcolm*: We shall not spend a large expense of time
> Before we reckon with your several loves,
> And make us even with you:...
>   ...this, and what needful else
> That calls upon us, by the grace of Grace,
> We will perform.   v, viii, 54–73

The clearest detached statement of God's mercy made in the miracle cycles is their treatment of one story which is of particular interest because of a later parallel in Shakespeare's work; this is the story of *The Woman Taken in Adultery*. Its dramatic possibilities at a simple, naturalistic level were obviously clear to the early dramatists. In the *Ludus Coventriae* a vivid stage direction which follows the arrival of the accusers at the woman's house runs: 'hic juvenis quidam extra currit, indeploydo colligis non ligatis et braccas in manu tenens.' The dialogue closely follows the gospel narrative:

> *Jesus*: Where be thy foemen that did thee accuse
> Why have they left us two alone?
> *Mulier*: Because they could not themselves excuse
> With shame they fled hence every one.   ll. 265 ff.

The fact that Shakespeare, in *Measure for Measure*, places what may seem to us excessive emphasis on the need for the personal righteousness of a just judge and also deals with this problem—itself a universal one—so definitely in terms of sexual sin, may well be accounted for by the power of this story over his imagination.

By sermons and widely circulating books of popular instruction, the themes of sin, justice and mercy were continually restated in Elizabethan times, although the angle of vision gradually changed.

First the growth of Protestant thought led to the disappearance of the medieval references to the 'deeds of mercy', so prominent in the Doomsday plays and earlier Moralities. In the Edwardian Homily *Of The Salvation of Mankind* (1547) the writer—possibly Cranmer himself—declares:

Because all men be sinners and offenders against God and breakers of his law and commandments, therefore can no man by his own acts... be justified and made righteous before God, but every man is constrained to seek after another righteousness.... For all the good works that we can do be imperfect and therefore not able to deserve our justification, but our justification does come freely by the mercy of God.

This is a shift of emphasis which does not appear to have occurred in Shakespeare's thought, a point which is of significance in view of the development which will be traced in the last plays. Undoubtedly the Doomsday scenes and their successors in the moralities must have been deeply offensive to Protestants intoxicated by the new doctrine of justification by faith alone, and therefore they probably contributed much to the new Church's distrust of religious drama and to its gradual extinction during Elizabeth's reign. The new secular drama, however, maintained the traditional subject-matter of justice and mercy in its own way.

It is remarkable that none of the early Elizabethan plays deal with the theme of mercy at anything but a perfunctory level. In *Cambyses* (c. 1560),[1] Sisamnes the unjust deputy, unlike Angelo in a similar situation, pleads for mercy in vain:

> *Sisamnes*: O noble king forgive my fact;
> I yield to thy mercy.

But there is no conflict here; the 'bitter deputy' is inexorably condemned; mercy is not contemplated. The theme of mercy bought by a vicarious sacrifice makes an occasional appearance in early secular drama, and it occurs in this play, where Otian, the son of the unjust judge, begs in vain to be allowed to die for his father. In *Damon and Pythias* (1571)[2] the willingness of the two friends to die for each other produces the best scene of the play.

[1] *Dodsley's Old English Plays*, vol. IV, ed. by W. C. Hazlitt (1874).
[2] *Minor Elizabethan Drama*, vol. I, ed. by A. Thorndyke.

Here entereth Damon running, and stays the sword.
  Damon: Stay, stay, stay! for the king's advantage, stay!...
  Damon is the man.

But Pithias persists in his determination to save his friend's life from Justice by sacrificing his own.

  Pithias: My Damon, the gods forbid but we should agree;
    Therefore agree to this, let me perform the promise made for thee.
    Let me die for thee:...
                my desire is but friendly.
    Do me this honour, that fame may report triumphantly,
    That Pithias for his friend Damon was contented to die.

In far better plays than this the triviality with which a great medieval theme may be introduced, only to be dropped again unexploited, is frequently disappointing. In *Friar Bacon and Friar Bungay*[1] Greene handles a subject which challenges serious treatment but does not receive it. When Friar Bacon breaks his magic glass and repents of his necromancy he says:

    Yet, Bacon, cheere thee, drowne not in despaire:...
    Thinke Mercie sits where Justice holds her seate,
    And from those wounds those bloudie Jews did pierce,
    Which by thy magick oft did bleed a fresh,
    From thence for thee the dew of mercy drops.   v, i

The sentiments carry no ring of conviction and are never referred to again—indeed, one is tempted to think that they are introduced rather for the horror of the penultimate line than for any more valid reason. Men had not forgotten the dichotomy of Justice and Mercy central in the miracle plays, but in sixteenth-century drama it lay dormant until Shakespeare, with some apparent incongruity, brought it to life once more in *The Comedy of Errors*.[2]

In their treatment of the obverse theme, that of Justice, however, Elizabethan playwrights are much more successful. The drama had become secular, but Justice is still imagined with its old numinous quality, its divine sanction.

---

[1] *Plays and Poems of Robert Greene*, ed. by J. Churton Collins (Oxford, 1905), vol. II.
[2] Cf. below, pp. 91 f.

Appius and Virginia (1580)[1] stands out partly because of its particularly poor writing, but also because of some interesting parallels with Shakespearean plays. When Appius, the unjust judge, plots to ravish Virginia the stage direction runs:

Here let him make as though he went out[2] and let Conscience and Justice come out and let Conscience hold in his hand a lamp burning, and let Justice have a sword and hold it before Appius' breast.

Appius struggles as desperately as the bumping verse allows, and the action allotted here to Justice reminds one of the traditional stage business in which Hamlet presents a sword directly against Claudius' back when the king is attempting repentance. It too often appears inept on the modern stage, but it is at least possible that it has a long stage ancestry, for of the many roles played by Hamlet that of Justice is among the most important. There are also links between *Appius and Virginia* and two other of Shakespeare's plays. The murder of the violated Virginia by her father recalls *Titus Andronicus*, and Appius' sin is attempted by another apparently just judge, Angelo. It is possible, therefore, that Shakespeare remembered the figure of Justice with his sword and instructed Burbage accordingly, but of course even if the business is Elizabethan in origin the action may have been no more than a stage commonplace.

King Cambises in his death out-herods Herod, of whom he is perhaps the earliest avatar in secular drama. He dies in his own 'vein', as Bottom would appreciate, and by accidentally killing himself illustrates justice in an ironic form particularly dear to Elizabethan hearts.

Enter the king, without a gowne, a sword thrust up into his side, bleeding.
King: Out alas? what shall I do? My life is finished;...
Is there noughte to be my help? nor is there nought to serve?...
Who but I in such a wise his death's wound could have got?
As I on horse-back up did leap, my sword from scabberd shot,
And run me thus into the side, as you right well may see...
Thus gasping here on ground I lie, for nothing I do care

---

[1] *Dodsley's Old English Plays*, vol. IV.   [2] = as though he would go out.

A just reward for my misdeeds my life doth plain declare.
Heere let him quake and stir.
Ambidexter: ...He cannot speak but beholde, how with Death he
doth strive.

Most Elizabethan tragedies can be classified as 'tragedies of blood',[1] and most of these are deeply concerned with the problems of Justice. However remote from the old religious tradition they may appear to be, their secular subject-matter does not obscure the essentially religious nature of the conception of justice which they embody. This Justice is clearly *Rightwyseness* in her scarlet robe demanding the rigour of the law, and she is equally clearly a Daughter of God. A very few examples must be accepted in illustration of this: one is the play *Arden of Feversham*,[2] which tells the story of a 'sex murder', with plenty of realistic contemporary incident and crude but vivid characterisation. The murderers and their accomplices are finally arrested by the mayor on circumstantial evidence and executed by due process of law, but this efficient working of the state machine is not the source of the play's sombre power. Supernatural sanctions operate as well as human ones. After the murder there occurs this scrap of dialogue:

Alice: Susan, fetch water and wash away this blood.
Susan: The blood cleaveth to the ground and will not out.
Alice: But with my nails I'll scrape away the blood;—
　　　The more I strive, the more the blood appears.　　　v, i

One after another the murderers betray themselves and work their own undoing. Alice Arden's own words first create suspicion of her:

Mosbie: Mistress Arden, here's to your husband.
Alice: My husband!
Franklyn: What ails you, woman, to cry so suddenly?　　　v, i

In a similar way the servant fails to destroy the blood-stained knife and dagger which are evidence against him and his mistress:

　　　I was so afraid I knew not what I did:
　　　I thought I had thrown them both into the well.[3]　　　v, i

---

[1] Edgar Stoll, *John Webster* (1905).
[2] *Minor Elizabethan Drama*, vol. I, ed. by A. Thorndyke.
[3] Cf. Abel's blood crying for vengeance: see above, p. 76.

This belief in the numinous working of divine justice affected even Marlowe—in his technique at least—since he ensures that Barabbas falls into his own cauldron and relates the unspeakably horrible death of Edward II to the particular nature of his 'sin', as indeed did Holinshed before him. It is the same essentially simple view of Justice as is voiced by Escalus at the end of *Romeo and Juliet*.

> See, what a scourge is laid upon your hate,
> That heaven finds means to kill your joys with love.
> And I for winking at your discords too
> Have lost a brace of kinsmen: all are punish'd.   v, iii, 292–5

The fascination exercised on Elizabethan audiences by the pattern typical of a 'revenge' play has been variously explained. For the scholarly of those days the machinery of such plots certainly carried the sign-manual of classical authority, and to the man-in-the-street the failure of the nation's courts to give certain justice to those victimised by either wealth or authority gave the search for redress a topical significance. Nevertheless, an explanation stemming from the native theatrical tradition is adequate to explain the affection felt by simple people for these plays. Until the presentation of *Tamburlaine* in 1588 the greatest tragic drama in existence in England was still in the miracle cycles whose climax was the Doomsday play, heralded by the trumpets of the archangels and completed with the gathering of the Saved and the Damned into Heaven and Hell. Such 'justice' must have been both desired and expected at the end of a play, and here secular drama faced a dilemma. Christian teaching was clear: 'Vengeance is mine; I will repay, saith the Lord',[1] yet in the new theatres, if divine justice were to be made visible, it had to be wreaked by the hand of man. Hence comes Hamlet's plea that he must be the 'Scourge and Minister' of Heaven, and that when he is able to send Rosencrantz and Guildenstern to their deserved deaths, 'even in that was heaven ordinant'. To claim such a role did not in itself suffice to make the avenger acceptable to Christian orthodoxy, but Thomas

---

[1] Romans, XII, 19.

Kyd in *The Spanish Tragedy* (*c.* 1590)[1] made of current belief a formula which, while leaving the execution of justice to a human agent, yet placed it squarely within the pattern of an ordered creation where the Creator's purposes were certain of fulfilment. Popular morality was happy to accept such myths as that Cassius committed suicide with the very sword with which he had stabbed Caesar, and that the atheist Marlowe was killed by his own hand thrusting his dagger into his eye. So in Kyd's play, which sets the pattern for all the following 'revenge' plays, including *Hamlet*, the engineer is expertly hoist with his own petard. Lorenzo, confident in his villainy, boasts:

> Nor shall they live for me to fear their faith,
> I'll trust myself, myself shall be my friend.
>
> The Spanish Tragedy, III, ii, 117–18

But he discovers too late that he cannot isolate himself from the world into which he is born. The laws of the universe are against him. 'Revenge' knows this and therefore preaches patience to Andrea's ghost:

> Thou talk'st of harvest, when the corn is green:
> The end is crown of every work well done;
> *The sickle comes not till the corn be ripe.*
> Be still;
>
> II, vi, 7–10

Isabella, in spite of her grief for her son, explicitly submits to time and the will of heaven:

> *The heavens are just*, murder cannot be hid;
> Time is the author of both truth and right,
> And time will bring this treachery to light.
>
> II, v, 57–9

Hieronimo accepts the duty of avenging Horatio, but he also believes that justice is ultimately in the hand of God not man.

> *Vindicta mihi.*
> Ay heaven will be revenged of every ill;
> Nor will they suffer murder unrepaid.
> Then stay Hieronimo, attend their will,
> For mortal man may not appoint their time.
>
> III, xiii, 1–5

[1] *The Spanish Tragedy*, ed. by Philip Edwards (Methuen, 1959).

A little later, however, he refuses to continue in the patience he had earlier professed and plans his own vengeance. The fiendish cunning with which he achieves the deaths of his foes has been held[1] to alienate sympathy from him. It marks, so this line of criticism runs, his metamorphosis into an Italianate villain, and this in turn accounts not only for the sinister method of the vengeance but also for the orgy of pointless bloodshed which follows his masque. This is a cogent argument, but to the present writer it does not appear to correspond to the imaginative impact of the play. The feigned friendship is very lightly touched upon: as to the killing of Lorenzo and Balthazar 'the justice of it pleases', and moreover it is immediately followed by one of Hieronimo's most appealing speeches as he tells of the death of his son and shows his body to the court. The horrors that follow are certainly revolting, but their very pointlessness—there is no secret still to be revealed when Hieronimo ensures silence by biting out his tongue—makes one believe that they are either an attempt to represent mania or else are piled up merely from a love of sensational stagecraft, and that it is unwarrantable to seek among them for any particular ethical significance.[2] The avenger, 'hesitating and irresolute in the face of overpowering evil',[3] finally achieves justice, but he does so in a situation which the villain himself in the ineluctable processes of time creates for his own undoing. Lorenzo plans the situation in which he perishes, just as Claudius plans the fencing match and the poisoned cup which lead him to his own death. The pattern is that of Peripeteia, or 'working in blindness to one's own defeat',[4] but it was used in England long before writers rediscovered the Poetics. The damned in the Doomsday plays had, like the saved, been free to perform the 'deeds of mercy' or to refrain from them. They chose to refrain, not in ignorance but in a self-imposed blindness to the significance of what they knew.

When was it that we saw thee sick, alas?

[1] F. T. Bowers, *English Revenge Tragedy* (1940).

[2] P. Edwards argues that the gratuitous horrors form part of a later, alternative version. See Preface to Edwards' edition of *The Spanish Tragedy*, p. xxxvi.

[3] *Minor Elizabethan Drama*, vol. I, ed. by Ashley Thornton, p. ix.

[4] F. L. Lucas, *Tragedy* (Hogarth Press, 1928).

G

> When did we this unkindliness?
> Weary or wet to let thee pass
> When did we thee this wickedness?   *Doomsday*

Centuries of Christian teaching had conditioned learned and simple alike to accept the story of the universe as a 'divine comedy'. Elizabethans believed that the end of such a play as *The Spanish Tragedy* mirrored truly the world in which they lived: to them the happy ending, which later became a melodramatic cliché, was still a statement of fact, a symbol which told of the working of God's Providence, and which could, in a shifting and threatening existence, offer an assurance of security.[1] In the words of *The Mirrour for Magistrates*:[2]

> Yet God, that suffereth silence to beguile
> Such guilts, wherewith both earth and air ye file,
> At last descries them to your foul deface,
> You see the examples set before your face.
>
> *The Complaint of Henry Duke of Buckingham*, stanza 19

Yet the conflict between the obligation to exact justice for a wrong done, and the contradictory obligation to forgive it, remained, and the pattern of events which appealed so strongly to popular consciousness was formed so as to include the payment by the avenger of his own life for his adversary's, albeit he had killed righteously. Kyd was sufficiently under the influence of Seneca to allow Hieronimo to take his own life, but later writers of 'revenge' plays spared the hero the guilt of suicide, arranging that he should fall by the hands of his enemies during the performance of his appointed task, as Hamlet is allowed to do.

The relative importance given to Justice and Mercy in early Elizabethan drama obtains also in Shakespeare's early work, but the balance is gradually adjusted until in his last plays it is reversed, and, as in the dialogue of the Vices and Virtues, Mercy is held supreme.

---

[1] The simplicity of such a faith does not appear in the later 'revenge' plays, e.g. those by Chapman and Webster, where its place is taken by interest in such things as the ethics and etiquette of the duel, machiavellism, stoicism and the villain-hero. Middleton does, however, recapture the old moral force in *The Changeling*.

[2] *Poetical Works of Thomas Sackville* (London, 1820).

2. THE DEBATE

The Comedy of Errors; *The Merchant of Venice*; *A Midsummer-Night's Dream*; *Romeo and Juliet*; *Henry V*; *Troilus and Cressida*; *The Two Gentlemen of Verona*

Some reference to the conflict between Justice and Mercy—so consistently pursued in medieval drama and so strangely neglected in the earlier secular plays—occurs in Shakespeare's earliest comedy; his treatment of it develops steadily until the theme is given its most magnificent statements in the great tragedies, and it continues to echo and re-echo through the last romances. Justice and Mercy are each, as Shakespeare shows, a true 'daughter of God', but the plays can leave no one in doubt as to which is the more lovely in his eyes. Man's true need, as Lear learnt at such cost, is not justice but mercy, yet this dichotomy seems for a time to have engendered such a tension in Shakespeare's imagination that it became a 'King Charles's head' appearing in unlikely places, giving unexpected overtones to pedestrian phrases and evoking similar emotions in widely different situations.

It is convenient to consider the plays preceding the tragedies in three groups; first comes the series which begins with *The Comedy of Errors* and culminates in *The Merchant of Venice*. Next come the plays containing mockery or serious criticism of the human institutions for effecting justice. Lastly there is *Measure for Measure* which, though it is alluded to earlier, demands separate treatment as it subsumes almost all the earlier thought on the subject and by bringing it into relation with new matter prepares the way for the later statements. It is noticeable that in the earlier plays Shakespeare seems to have conceived of the conflict primarily in its social context, and that some attempt is made in very diverse situations to suggest a pragmatic solution. These first treatments attempt to resolve the problem by allotting the function of justice to the state while reserving the duties of mercy and forgiveness to the individual.

The Comedy of Errors, in the main a Plautian farce of riotous good spirits, begins in a court of law where a man is on trial for his life. We may—quite legitimately—resent having our sympathies roused on his behalf when the play as a whole demands no such responses, but apparently Shakespeare could not himself resist the appeal of that imagined figure, a lonely foreigner facing a hostile judge. Perhaps he remembered him years later when writing of another alien, a Jew of Venice; in any case the voices in the two courts echo each other.

> *Duke of Ephesus*: Again, if any Syracusian born
>   Come to the bay of Ephesus, he dies,
>   His goods confiscate to the duke's dispose.
>
> *Comedy of Errors*, I, i, 19–21

> *Portia*:   thy lands and goods
>   Are, by the laws of Venice, confiscate
>   Unto the state of Venice
>
> *Merchant of Venice*, IV, i, 310–12

> *Duke of Ephesus*: Unless a thousand marks be levied,
>   To quit the penalty...
>   Beg thou, or borrow, to make up the sum.
>
> I, i, 22–3, 154

> *Shylock*: I cannot instantly raise up the gross   I, iii, 56

> *Antonio*:   thou mayst with better face
>   Exact the penalty.   I, iii, 137–8

The Duke of Ephesus states for the first time the contemporary dictum which Shakespeare was content to use in the earlier plays:

> Now, trust me, were it not against our laws,
> Against my crown, my oath, my dignity,
> Which princes, would they, may not disannul,
> My soul should sue as advocate for thee.
> For we may pity, though not pardon thee.
>
> *Comedy of Errors*, I, i, 143–6, 98

There does also appear with it the Christian concept that the debt to justice may be paid vicariously:

> Yet once again proclaim it publicly,
> If any friend will pay the sum for him
> He shall not die.   V, i, 130–2

This is of course exactly what Shylock, in his purblind insistence on the old law, will not admit. Still, in the absence of payment the responsibilities of the state demand the strict fulfilment of its statutes. Even the gay *Midsummer-Night's Dream* opens with no less rigid a pronouncement, for Theseus himself bids Hermia marry according to her father's wish:

> Or else the law of Athens yields you up—
> Which by no means we may extenuate—
> To death, or to a vow of single life.   I, i, 119–21

In *Romeo and Juliet* Duke Escalus gives the justification for such severity when he has declared his irrevocable fiat to the citizens:

> Mercy but murders, pardoning those that kill.   III, i, 202

After Tybalt is killed Lady Capulet demands from Escalus what Friar Laurence calls 'the rigour of severest law' (v, i, 269):

> For blood of ours, shed blood of Montague...
> I beg for justice, which thou, prince, must give;
> Romeo slew Tybalt, Romeo must not live.   III, i, 154–86

Escalus, however, takes into account that the man slain by Romeo was himself the aggressor, and Friar Laurence declares:

> Thy fault our law calls death; but the kind prince,
> Taking thy part, hath rush'd aside the law,
> And turn'd that black word death to banishment;
> This is dear mercy.

But Romeo can only answer:

> 'Tis torture, and not mercy.   III, iii, 25–9

Indeed his punishment, though perfectly legal, appears to ordinary vision both an unjust and an inept way of dealing with a human dilemma, and there seems to be more true justice as well as more humanity in the action of Theseus, who, when he discovers that Aegeus intends to give his daughter to a man who neither wants her nor loves her, is prepared to set aside legality.

> Egeus, I will overbear your will;
> For in the temple, by and by, with us

These couples shall eternally be knit.

Midsummer-Night's Dream, IV, i, 183-5

The particular situation in which Theseus is prepared thus to 'wrest once the law' to his authority may be not without significance. Mutuality in love appears to have been an overriding value in Shakespeare's eyes. It was in part what distinguished Romeo's love for Juliet from his love for Rosaline:

> she whom I love now
> Doth grace for grace and love for love allow.   II, iii, 85-6

It is apparently one of the factors that promote human love into a value to which all else—even justice herself—must be subservient.

The conception of the king's function as a mediator between the individual and the law is treated more seriously in *Henry V*, who seems in this respect to support the Duke of Athens in allowing personal discretion in the administration of justice.

> *K. Henry:*   Uncle of Exeter,
> Enlarge the man committed yesterday,
> That rail'd against our person: we consider
> It was excess of wine that set him on;
> And on his more advice we pardon him.
>
> *Henry V*, II, ii, 39-43

When, a moment after, he faces Scroop and the other traitors the shield is reversed.

> The mercy which was quick in us but late,
> By your own counsel is suppress'd and kill'd:...
>   Get you therefore hence,
> Poor miserable wretches, to your death.   II, ii, 79-80, 177-8

The necessity for compromise in society was of course well known to the Elizabethan political theorists; it underlies the common belief that a prince, whose position allowed him to override the law, was the subjects' chief safeguard against oppression, and Professor Sisson has demonstrated that in Shakespeare's England the current conflict between case-law and the law of the king's prerogative courts was a major social issue. The distinction between written law and law on the lips of a supreme ruler does not appear, however, to have interested Shakespeare deeply.

In *Troilus and Cressida* Shakespeare puts into the mouth of Hector a magnificent statement concerning the nature of the law which the state should exist to enforce. It is based on the relationship between human and divine law, for to Renaissance man the 'law of nature' was still a direct reflection of the absolute law of God.

> If this law
> Of nature be corrupted through affection,
> And that great minds, of partial indulgence
> To their benumbed wills, resist the same,
> There is a law in each well-ordered nation
> To curb those raging appetites that are
> Most disobedient and refractory.
> If Helen then be wife to Sparta's king,
> As it is known she is, these moral laws
> Of nature and of nations speak aloud
> To have her back return'd.   II, ii, 176–86

But the law of nations does not always fulfil the function that Hector so lucidly describes. The Venice of Antonio the Merchant exists by legally enforcing the violation of those laws of nature which the laws of human society should reflect. A man there lives by taking a 'breed for barren metal of his friend', by making gold and silver breed as fast as ewes and rams, and in his eyes a bond which has no relationship to the law of nature is yet held sacred. The laws are enforced so that profits can be made from trade, and Antonio admits it as readily as Shylock. Falconbridge's 'tickling commodity' has become a cornerstone of the state.

> *Antonio*: The duke cannot deny the course of law:
> For the commodity that strangers have
> With us in Venice, if it be denied,
> Will much impeach the justice of the state:
> Since that the trade and profit of the city
> Consisteth of all nations.
>   *Merchant of Venice*, III, iii, 26–31

The nature of such a conception of law becomes clearer if we imagine it applied in Belmont; there it would be shown up as at once superficial and unnecessary. In Belmont men like the princes of Morocco and Aragon, who assess to a nicety their own deserts, can never 'win the fleece', and success will come only to a man who claims nothing for himself but is ready 'to give and hazard all he hath', not 'in hope of fair advantages', but without any promise of return. A different law, clearly recognised by Portia's father on his death-bed—'Holy men at their death have good inspirations' as Nerissa says—runs in this land. By it love wins both wealth and happiness while selfishness and arrogance miss them. It is a different law from that of Venice, as much more exacting in its penalties as it is generous in its rewards.

In *The Merchant of Venice* the court, no less than Shylock himself, stands throughout for the enforcement of a law which is of 'nations' though not of 'nature'. When an attempt is made to abrogate it, even for a moment, the answer comes immediately in Portia's own words:

> It must not be: there is no power in Venice
> Can alter a decree established:
> 'Twill be recorded for a precedent,
> And many an error by the same example
> Will rush into the state.   IV, i, 218–22

It has been suggested that Portia does, in fact, 'wrest the law' to her authority, and that Shylock is in reality foiled, not by her legal quibbles, but by the serene goodness, the fresh commonsense that, in her own person, she brings into the alien world of Venice. John Russell Brown, the editor of the New Arden edition of the play, who puts forward this view, supports it by showing that Victor Sylvaine in *The Orator*, 1596, successfully demolishes the legality of Portia's defence. It may well be that the young lawyers of the Inns of Court realised the weakness of her case, but there is nothing whatever in the play to suggest that to evoke such an interpretation was Shakespeare's intention. On the contrary, the structure and tension of the trial scene depend on the complete peripeteia which occurs when he who invokes the law perishes by the law. It would be impossible to persuade an audience at a successful theatrical performance to allow any different reading to override this one. Shylock's fall may be tragic, or it may be grotesquely comic, but its significance must always depend on the literal fulfilment of his own blindly self-confident words:

> My deeds upon my head! I crave the law,
> The penalty and forfeit of my bond.   IV, i, 206–7

Portia herself accepts the unequivocal and absolute demands of the law and makes no attempt to influence their application. Her appeals for mercy are addressed not to the court but to the individuals concerned:

> Then must the Jew be merciful   IV, i, 182

And later:

> What mercy can *you* render *him*,[1] Antonio? IV, i, 378

The plot of the play and the language of the appeal make it perfectly clear not only that it was right for Shylock and Antonio to show mercy, but also that it was right for the court to offer justice. There is no suggestion that the duke was wrong not to curb a 'cruel devil of his will' by illegal means, and Antonio, an older and wiser man than either Bassanio or Gratiano, never expects, nor apparently desires, such a thing. The second Venetian law, to which Portia finally appeals, specifically states that the offender's life 'lies in the mercy of the duke only', so that the duke is given a prerogative which he may legally exercise by offering what Isabella was later to call 'lawful mercy'. Antonio, on the other hand, grants Shylock his life and remits his share of Shylock's wealth as a purely individual act of mercy, and his generosity is not flawed by his insistence on the unwilling conversion to Christianity. The Elizabethans undoubtedly accepted as normal Gratiano's eager desire for the sport of a public hanging, together with the drawing and quartering that went with it; to them Antonio's proviso would appear a pious offer of possible salvation, and Shakespeare must have expected this reaction whether or not he shared it.

On what grounds do we find that Shakespeare actually bases the plea for mercy? Perhaps, in the first place, on the intrinsic loveliness of mercy in itself.

---

[1] Italics the author's.

> *Portia*: It droppeth as the gentle rain from heaven
> Upon the place beneath:...
>> it becomes
> The throned monarch better than his crown.   IV, i, 185–9

Beyond this is the urgent sense of the individual's own continual need for mercy from his God and his certainty of obtaining it should he repent. As early as *Titus Andronicus* Shakespeare allows Tamora (somewhat out of character certainly) to voice this faith using a contemporary aphorism:

> Wilt thou draw near the nature of the gods?
> Draw near them then in being merciful.   I, i, 117–18

In *The Two Gentlemen of Verona*, Valentine applies the axiom to his own conduct.

> Who by repentance is not satisfied
> Is nor of heaven nor earth, for these are pleased.
> By penitence the Eternal's wrath's appeased: v, iv, 79–81

From such simple beginnings grew the great lines of the later plays:

>> the rarer action is
> In virtue than in vengeance: they being penitent,
> The sole drift of my purpose doth extend
> Not a frown further.
>
>> *The Tempest*, v, i, 27–30

> Why, all the souls that were were forfeit once;
> And He that might the vantage best have took
> Found out the remedy.
>
>> *Measure for Measure*, II, ii, 67–9

If we interpret the trial at Venice at its deepest level, I believe that we can hear, through Portia, the voice of God himself pleading with mankind to accept the offered remedy. If Shylock had done so he would have saved his own soul, so much more profitable an undertaking to him than the gaining of Antonio's life. When Shylock demands to know on what compulsion he must be merciful, Portia gives him first the answer as she understands it—the quality of mercy is not strained; there can be no compulsion, but

> we do pray for mercy;
> And that same prayer doth teach us all to render
> The deeds of mercy.   IV, i, 200–2

When he refuses this plea, she uses with an exquisite humility his own language, so that by any means he may be saved:

> Shylock, there's thrice thy money offer'd thee.   IV, i, 227

Failing again, she attempts next to shock him into a realisation of the horror of what he is doing. When she makes this third attempt to win him the whole force of the lines should be directed at him, not at Antonio or the public:

> lawfully by this the Jew may claim
> A pound of flesh, to be by him cut off
> Nearest the merchant's heart. Be merciful:
> Take thrice thy money; bid me tear the bond. IV, i, 231–4

She should, I believe, still watch Shylock as she tells Antonio to prepare for death; it is not yet too late. Even her burst of anger when he will admit no obligation to provide a surgeon—

> It is not so express'd; but what of that?
> 'Twere good you do so much for charity.   IV, i, 260–1

—is a last effort to shame him into a retreat from the trap into which he is hastening. But nothing avails, and after this Portia stops thinking of Shylock and considers only Antonio, until the instant that the trap has actually to be sprung: 'Tarry a little; there is something else.' For Portia has not claimed that earthly power is likest God's when it shows nothing but mercy: the image of Doomsday was not yet forgotten.

3. SOCIAL JUSTICE

Measure for Measure; *The Comedy of Errors*; *2 Henry IV*; *Henry V*; *Much Ado about Nothing*; *Henry VIII*; *Troilus and Cressida*

In the comedies of the middle period and in the comic scenes of the history plays the pretensions of the state to administer justice are reflected in either the 'steel glass' of satire or the distorting mirror of farce, and the inadequacy of the human instrument which is thus exposed proves to be an intrinsic part of the problem, for the Duke of Vienna voices an impossible demand when he says:

> He who the sword of heaven will bear
> Should be as holy as severe;
>
> *Measure for Measure*, III, ii, 275–6

and the law is too often made ridiculous by its ministers. The prototype of all the comic officers of the law is the constable of Ephesus who arrests Antipholus. He is evidently a poor, weak creature who tries to keep out of trouble by placating prisoner and would-be rescuers alike, but he is given a worthy exit.

> *Enter* ANTIPHOLUS *with his rapier drawn*
> *Luciana*: God, for thy mercy! they are loose again.
> *Adriana*: And come with naked swords....
> *Officer*: Away! they'll kill us.
> [*Exeunt omnes as fast as may be, frighted.*[1]
>
> *Comedy of Errors*, IV, iv, 147–50

A constable who may well be taken more seriously is Elbow, for, in spite of his difficulty in expressing himself, he is a shrewd enough judge of people and places in Vienna to be an efficient officer.

> If it please your honour, I am the poor duke's constable, and my name is Elbow: I do lean upon justice, sir, and do bring in here before your good honour two notorious benefactors.... If it please your honour, I know not well what they are: but precise villains they are, that I am sure of; and void of all profanation in the world that good Christians ought to have....He, sir! a tapster, sir; parcel-bawd; one that serves a bad woman;...I say, sir, that this house, if it be not a bawd's house, it is pity of her life, for it is a naughty house.
>
> *Measure for Measure*, II, i, 47–78

A difficult witness, no doubt, but he comes out of their interview more creditably than does the impatient Angelo, and his 'leaning upon justice' was more genuine and far less harmful than his superior's.

---

[1] Stage direction in Folio.

The razor-edge between farce and tragedy is apparent in the arrest of Doll and Quickly while Falstaff is at the wars. The representative of the law certainly suffers severely at Doll's tongue, and his appearance is very clearly indicated as grotesque in the extreme.

Doll: Nut-hook, nut-hook, you lie....thou damned tripe-visaged rascal...thou paper-faced villain...you thin man in a censer...you blue-bottle rogue, you filthy famished correctioner...Goodman death, goodman bones!   *2 Henry IV*, v, iv, 8–32

The women do not escape him, however, and it is his words which set the tone for the scene:

...Come, I charge you both go with me; for the man is dead that you and Pistol beat amongst you.   v, iv, 18–19

We are reminded of the provost in *Measure for Measure* speaking of Claudio and Barnardine:

> The one has my pity; not a jot the other,
> Being a murderer, though he were my brother.
>
>   IV, ii, 64–5

The law is fair game in slighter situations, but when a man's life is involved it is best taken seriously. There is nothing in the writing to suggest, for example, that Shakespeare found it amusing that Bardolph should at last be hanged for stealing a 'pax', nor that he invited us to share Fluellen's approval of the king who condemned his old boon companion.

Pistol: But Exeter hath given the doom of death,
  For pax of little price....
Speak, captain, for his life, and I will thee requite.
Fluellen: Auncient Pistol, I do partly understand your meaning.
Pistol: Why then, rejoice therefore.
Fluellen: Certainly auncient, it is not a thing to rejoice at; for if, look you, he were my brother, I would desire the duke to use his good pleasure, and put him to execution; for discipline ought to be used....
King Henry: What men have you lost, Fluellen?
Fluellen: ...I think the duke hath lost never a man, but one that is like

to be executed for robbing a church, one, Bardolph, if your majesty
know the man:...
King Henry: We would have all offenders so cut off.

Henry V, III, vi, 45–116

Pistol's cheerful assumption that any chance of easy money is a
cause for rejoicing meets Fluellen's belief that to further the course
of justice is more important than to gain a living. King Henry
stands with the fanatical Welshman, but his figure is seen from a
more probing angle of vision. The price of justice may be not to
forgo a quick profit but to forget a friend. 'If your majesty know
the man', says Fluellen, and the king does not answer him. There
is no overt criticism, but the problem is for a moment shown in
depth, and with the depth comes doubt. Pistol's terse comment is
hard to rebut:

and figo for thy friendship!... The fig of Spain! III, vi, 60–2

At the other end of the scale comes the Lord Chief Justice himself
who has to bear a juxtaposition with Falstaff from which he does
not escape scot-free. Speaking to the young King Henry V he
clearly stated his own function.

Your highness pleased to forget my place,
The majesty and power of law and justice,
The image of the king whom I presented.

2 Henry IV, v, ii, 77–9

Since, then, the judge is the image of the king and the king the
image of God, it is evident that the justice dispensed in an earthly
court of law ought to be an image of the heavenly justice dispensed
by God. In the historical plays, however, Shakespeare gives no
prominent place to any conception of absolute justice and continues to be concerned with a wry enjoyment of the inadequacy of
even the greatest of the human instruments who purvey justice in
society. In the three-cornered conversation following his rebuke
by the Lord Chief Justice, it is Falstaff who scores highest.

Falstaff: My lord, this is a poor mad soul; and she says up and down the
town, that her eldest son is like you:...   II, i, 113–15

But to Shakespeare thoughts of justice do not easily remain within the framework of comedy; the ambiguous ending of *2 Henry IV* suggests a more sinister criticism than Falstaff's. After the new king has dismissed his disreputable friends, allowing them competence for life and the chance of advancement, the Lord Chief Justice immediately returns. He apparently acts on his own authority, for the text gives no further words to the king, and although his courage and integrity have recently disposed us to an unexpected sympathy, we do not forget his earlier discomfiture:

This is the right fencing grace, my lord; tap for tap, and so part fair.
                                                                    II, i, 205

There were other scores to settle as well:

God give your lordship good time of day.... I heard say your lordship was sick: I hope your lordship goes abroad by advice. Your lordship, though not clean past your youth, hath yet some smack of age in you, some relish of the saltness of time; and I most humbly beseech your lordship to have a reverent care of your health....   I, ii, 109–15

Falstaff triumphed twice, but it is dangerous to challenge authority.

Go, carry Sir John Falstaff to the Fleet.   v, v, 97–8

This appears to be the use of power in pursuit of personal vengeance; the implications are not flattering to the Lord Chief Justice, and it is not he but his victim who is given Mistress Quickly's exquisite epitaph:

Quickly: ...He's in Arthur's bosom, if ever man went to Arthur's
    bosom.   *Henry V*, II, iii, 9–10

Shakespeare apparently enjoyed contemplating the humbler minions of the law rather than the greater, for he makes them much more likeable people. Dogberry, if he had been placed higher on the legal ladder, would not have hesitated to commit his prince for contempt of his 'very seat of judgment'.

Dost thou not suspect my place? dost thou not suspect my years?... I am a wise fellow, and, which is more, an officer, and, which is more, ...as pretty a piece of flesh as any is in Messina, and one that knows the law, go to...and a fellow that hath had losses....
                          Much Ado about Nothing, IV, ii, 76–87

He might have had a moment of hesitation—'Write down Prince John a villain. Why, this is flat perjury, to call a prince's brother villain'—but who can doubt that righteous indignation would have overcome it? We cannot believe, however, that Dogberry would wantonly have committed Falstaff to the Fleet; he has the invaluable testimony of his partner to the contrary.

Verges: You have always been called a merciful man, partner.
Dogberry: Truly, I would not hang a dog by my will, much more a man
who hath any honesty in him.   III, iii, 65–8

This is more than Shakespeare would allow most purveyors of justice to claim, and perhaps his most vivid summing up of what a man can hope to receive in a court of law is given by Henry VIII when the king warns Cranmer of the trap laid for him by the Privy Council. The tone may occasionally be bantering, but the matter is deadly serious.

>   Know you not
> How your state stands i' the world, with the whole world?
> Your enemies are many, and not small; their practices
> Must bear the same proportion; and not ever
> The justice and the truth o' the question carries
> The due o' the verdict with it: at what ease
> Might corrupt minds procure knaves as corrupt
> To swear against you? such things have been done.
> You are potently opposed; and with a malice
> Of as great size. Ween you of better luck,
> I mean, in perjured witness, than your master,
> Whose minister you are, whiles here he lived
> Upon this naughty earth? Go to, go to;
> You take a precipice for no leap of danger,
> And woo your own destruction.

>   *Henry VIII*, v, i, 126–40

In *Troilus and Cressida* Shakespeare presents pictures both of what human justice should be and of what it in fact too often is. Ulysses, posing as the expositor of Order, describes the chaos that follows the taking away of Degree thus:

> Force should be right; or rather, right and wrong,
> Between whose endless jar justice resides,

Should lose their names, and so should justice too.

Troilus and Cressida, I, iii, 115-17

The speech as a whole is so persuasive that these lines have
sometimes been held to express Shakespeare's own conception of
justice, but such an interpretation is quite inadmissible. The man
who utters these words is not himself a lord in any ordered hierarchy. He is a crafty 'dog-fox' who, like Polonius, would 'by in-
directions find directions out'. He works by fomenting the very
factiousness he decries, for he plays off Ajax against Achilles, and
Achilles against Ajax, while he inflames the vanity of his leaders as
skilfully as he does that of their followers. He invokes the

> envious fever
> Of pale and bloodless emulation   I, iii, 133-4

although he appears to condemn its ruthless methods, for he urges
Achilles on with the words:

> For honour travels in a strait so narrow,
> Where one but goes abreast: keep then the path;
> For emulation hath a thousand sons
> That one by one pursue: if you give way,
> Or hedge aside from the direct forthright,
> Like to an enter'd tide, they all rush by
> And leave you hindmost.   III, iii, 154-60

In a society so motivated by competition and self-interest it may be
useful to compel a compromise between opposing forces but to call
such a thing justice is merely equivocal.

There is, however, another political theorist in the play whose
vision is different from that of Ulysses. Hector, whose analysis of
natural and man-made law we have already considered, describes
justice thus:

> Nature craves
> All dues be render'd to their owners.   II, ii, 173-4

Here no point of balance between right and wrong is envisaged.
The value of such justice

> dwells not in particular will;
> It holds his estimate and dignity

H

> As well wherein 'tis precious of itself
> As in the prizer.   II, ii, 53-6

Yet just as Ulysses understands the beauty of order but lives by disrupting it, so Hector refuses to be guided by the justice which he recognises as real. After the lines concerning the obedience to law which would dictate the return of Helen to Menelaus, he continues:

> thus to persist
> In doing wrong extenuates not wrong,
> But makes it much more heavy. Hector's opinion
> Is this in way of truth; yet ne'ertheless,
> My spritely brethren, I propend to you
> In resolution to keep Helen still,
> For 'tis a cause that hath no mean dependance
> Upon our joint and several dignities.   II, ii, 186-93

Like Portia's Prince of Aragon he shares the 'one touch of nature' which

> makes the whole world kin,
> That all with one consent praise new-born gawds, ...
> And give to dust that is a little gilt
> More laud than gilt o'er-dusted.   III, iii, 175-9

That is to say he rejects the world of reality where value 'dwells not in particular will' and enters the world of *appearances*, where Troilus naturally expects no answer to what he considers his rhetorical question:

> What is aught, but as 'tis valued?   II, ii, 52

Troilus learns to know this world well; in it the greatest 'goods'—love, mercy, chivalry—are all 'suffocate', along with Degree. Later he says to Hector:

> Brother, you have a vice of mercy in you,
> Which better fits a lion than a man.
> *Hector:* What vice is that, good Troilus? chide me for it.
> *Troilus:* When many times the captive Grecian falls,
> Even in the fan and wind of your fair sword,
> You bid them rise, and live.
> *Hector:* O, 'tis fair play.

Troilus: Fool's play, by heaven, Hector...
Hector: Fie, savage, fie!   v, iii, 37–49

But Hector has deliberately chosen the amoral world where value is ignored and only appearances count, and in that world he dies. He fights on the battlefield wearing the armour of the actual 'savage', Achilles, which he has stripped from the dead body of Patroclus.

Hector: Most putrified core, so fair without,
Thy goodly armour thus hath cost thy life.
Now is my day's work done.   v, viii, 1–3

This 'goodly outside', which he has deliberately assumed, costs Hector his own life also, for as he doffs it Achilles and the Myrmidons appear, intent on their revenge.

Achilles: Look, Hector, how the sun begins to set;...
Hector: I am unarm'd: forego this vantage, Greek.
Achilles: Strike, fellows, strike: this is the man I seek....
On, Myrmidons, and cry you all amain.
'Achilles hath the might Hector slain.'   v, viii, 5–14

After the killing of Patroclus comes the killing of Hector: 'the endless jar' settles for a moment to rest, but it is not justice which is achieved. Hector has lost the 'dignity' he sacrificed his own knowledge of truth to gain, and Achilles has won it. Among men who sacrifice Truth to Appearance, Achilles may safely 'assume desert', but the world he moves in is a grim one:

Achilles: The dragon wing of night o'erspreads the earth,
And, stickler-like, the armies separates.
My half-supp'd sword, that frankly would have fed,
Pleased with this dainty bait, thus goes to bed.
v, viii, 17–20

Indeed, 'the cat will mew, the dog will have his day', but Shakespeare does not so abandon the problem of justice: he returns to it in *Measure for Measure,* and after the mockery of the Histories and the irony of *Troilus and Cressida* the change of mood is marked.

4. THE SWORD OF HEAVEN

Measure for Measure

At a first approach the likeness of *Measure for Measure* to *The Merchant of Venice* is striking, but in fact the thought of the later play has become subtilised into something quite distinct from any earlier statement. Isabella's plea for mercy is the supreme one. Shakespeare apparently never desires to word it again; he certainly never did so. It is a religious plea, as Portia's was; it considers no reasons, excuses or useful compromises. As God loved man without man's deserving and in spite of man's sin, so must man, needing mercy, offer it without reserve.[1]

> *Isabella:*   Well, believe this,
> No ceremony that to great ones 'longs,
> Not the king's crown, nor the deputed sword,
> The marshal's truncheon, nor the judge's robe,
> Become them with one half so good a grace
> As mercy does....
>   Alas, alas!
> Why, all the souls that were were forfeit once
> And He that might the vantage best have took
> Found out the remedy. How would you be,
> If He, which is the top of judgement, should
> But judge you as you are? O, think on that;
> And mercy then will breathe within your lips,
> Like man new made.   II, ii, 58–79

The imagery is important. Although man's dress of authority disguises the weakness inherent in him, yet Isabella still finds the panoply of human justice a beautiful thing. The robes, the truncheon, the deputed sword become their wearers well, though not so well as mercy does. She has not yet experienced the horror of discovering that such shows may be not merely insufficient, but actually deceptive and therefore hideous. When this revelation

---

[1] There is a vivid contrast to Shakespeare's attitude to be found at the end of *Volpone*:
Corvino and Voltore: We beg favour.
Celia: And mercy.
Avoci: You hurt your innocence suing for the guilty.

comes the play loses touch with *The Merchant of Venice* and shows its kinship with *King Lear*.

> Merciful Heaven,
> Thou rather with thy sharp and sulphurous bolt
> Split'st the unwedgeable and gnarled oak
> Than the soft myrtle: but man, proud man,
> Drest in a little brief authority,...
> Plays such fantastic tricks before high heaven
> As make the angels weep.   II, ii, 114–23

As Isabella sought mercy so, when her own ordeal comes, she offers it—not without an effort, but in the end completely. In the folk-tale situation of the play we do not doubt that Angelo's life might indeed be forfeit to her in requital for her brother's.

> *Duke*: Against all sense you do importune her:
> Should she kneel down in mercy of this fact,
> Her brother's ghost his paved bed would break,
> And take her hence in horror.
> *Mariana*:   Isabel,
> Sweet Isabel, do yet but kneel by me;
> Hold up your hands, say nothing; I'll speak all....
> Oh Isabel, will you not lend a knee?
> *Duke*: He dies for Claudio's death.   v, i, 438–48

After a silence which endures for forty-five lines of dialogue and as long a pause as the actress can sustain, Isabella does at last fulfil her own absolute demands: she kneels. 'Look ... on this man ... as if my brother lived.' That is all that is required of Isabella, but broken by grief, disappointment and loneliness she does not see the duke's silent acceptance of her plea; she stumbles on:

> I partly think
> A due sincerity govern'd his deeds,
> Till he did look on me: v, i, 450–2

It is quite true and not irrelevant: the search for the motive, the attempt to assess the degree of guiltiness, both are necessary in the social situation. But Isabella is not there to do social justice, she is there to forgive, and as she struggles to find further extenuation in the terms of a world in which she is not at home, she goes further astray.

> My brother had but justice,
> In that he did the thing for which he died:
> For Angelo,
> His act did not o'ertake his bad intent,
> And must be buried but as an intent
> That perish'd by the way: thoughts are no subjects;
> Intents but merely thoughts.   v, i, 153–9

Here Isabella is wrong. In the sermon which so clearly influenced this play we read:

Ye have heard that it was said by them of old time, Thou shalt not commit adultery: But I say unto you, That whosoever looketh on a woman to lust after her hath committed adultery with her already in his heart.[1]

The duke dismisses her plea.

> Your suit's unprofitable; stand up, I say.   v, i, 460

Angelo is forgiven not because his crimes were both in intent only, but because the duke hears and believes the words he speaks to Escalus:

> *Angelo*: I am sorry that such sorrow I procure:
> And so deep sticks it in my penitent heart
> That I crave death more willingly than mercy,
> 'Tis my deserving, and I do entreat it.   v, i, 479–82

Measure for Measure makes the full statement that to show mercy is the ultimate, ineluctable demand on the individual, without consideration of desert or excuse. What of the state? Should it consider any demand as absolute? If so, should it be the demand of justice or of mercy? Angelo, 'the voice of the recorded law', makes the same absolute demand for justice that Isabella makes for mercy. He puts forward the old pragmatic arguments for justice used by Antonio and Shylock, and he puts them well.

> *Angelo*: The law hath not been dead, though it hath slept:
> Those many had not dared to do that evil,

[1] Matthew v, 27–8.

> If the first that did the edict infringe
> Had answer'd for his deed:...
> *Isabella*:   Yet show some pity.
> *Angelo*: I show it most of all when I show justice;
> For then I pity those I do not know,
> Which a dismiss'd offence would after gall.   II, ii, 90–102

And he is consistent. Like Isabella he applies to himself the standards he had demanded of others. He asks for the punishment of death—'it is my deserving and I do entreat it'.

Not only however does Angelo fail to apply his ideal of justice, but, more important, the ideal itself is clearly shown as unacceptable within the total design of the play. It is refuted on three scores. Isabella voices her ultimate condemnation. Man should be like his Maker in seeking remedies to cure evil rather than in cutting it off. Man's original sin was the *Felix Culpa* from which his redemption stemmed, for:

> He that might the vantage best have took,
> Found out the remedy.   II, ii, 74–5

The duke however condemns Angelo's severity for an opposite reason. Angelo would be right to execute justice if he were himself without sin:

> ...his life is parallel'd
> Even with the stroke and line of his great justice:
> ...were he meal'd with that
> Which he corrects, then were he tyrannous;
> But this being so, he's just.   IV, ii, 82–8

This is a judgment made in the same absolute terms as Isabella's. In an ideal world—the world of Belmont for example—this proviso that the judge must be without sin would find unhesitating agreement: it is not so self-evident that one should accept it as axiomatic in the Vienna of Barnardine and Pompey, Lucio and Mistress Overdone. Isabella, and Angelo himself, do so accept it however. Isabella pleads:

> Go to your bosom;
> Knock there, and ask your heart what it doth know
> That's like my brother's fault: if it confess

III

> A natural guiltiness such as is his,
> Let it not sound a thought upon your tongue
> Against my brother's life.   II, ii, 136-41

Angelo in his soliloquy admits the justice of her plea.

> O, let her brother live:
> Thieves for their robbery have authority
> When judges steal themselves.   II, ii, 175-7

The duke sums up this position:

> He who the sword of heaven will bear
> Should be as holy as severe;...
> Shame to him whose cruel striking
> Kills for faults of his own liking!
> Twice treble shame on Angelo,
> To weed my vice and let his grow!   III, ii, 275-84

There is perfection when the moral law and the law of nations coincide, and when the administrator is himself sinless before the law. Such perfection cannot be expected among men, but though the personal morality of the judge is rationally irrelevant when the law itself is concerned not with moral values but with the stability of an amoral society, yet it remains even then emotionally important, because men *feel* in terms of right and wrong, even when they *act* in terms of expediency. Shakespeare is thus brought to an *impasse* for 'none is good but one, that is God'. On such a plane there is only one able to give sentence, the one who said to the woman taken in adultery: 'Go and sin no more.' And it has already been suggested that Shakespeare had this prototype in mind as he wrote *Measure for Measure*.

Apart from such considerations, however, it becomes obvious that Angelo, 'mealed with that which he corrects', ceases to carry out even his simplest judicial functions either efficiently or honestly. He asks to deal with Isabella and Mariana so that he may silence them, but even so he leaves their cross-examination to Escalus. His sin has 'unabled' him. Angelo's third group of critics stand throughout on such common sense criteria and make no absolute demands; they think it a waste that Claudio should die because he is a fine young man who can ill be spared, and so they make excuses for him and blame Angelo for his severity.

> *Escalus*: Let us be keen, and rather cut a little,
> Than fall, and bruise to death.　　　　　　　　　　II, i, 5–6

> *Provost*: All sects, all ages smack of this vice; and he
> To die for't!　　　　　　　　　　II, ii, 5–6

> *Provost*: It is a bitter deputy.　　　　　　　　　　IV, ii, 81

'Use every man after his desert, and who should 'scape whipping?' If men were offered consistent justice, society would disintegrate. Once more the germ of Shakespeare's later thought can be found in an early comedy. Berowne declares that the absolute fulfilment of absolute obligations is impossible for men, who can only claim:

> As true we are as flesh and blood can be.
> *Love's Labour's Lost*, IV, iii, 215

We are reminded of Falstaff: 'If sack and sugar be a fault, God help the wicked' (*1 Henry IV*, II, iv, 85), and of old Lafeu's words to Parolles: 'Though you are a fool and a knave, you shall eat' (*All's Well that Ends Well*, V, ii, 57).

In the world of relative values and practical problems Escalus, aided by the Provost and Constable Elbow, maintains some semblance of good order by compromises, warnings, threats, procrastination and occasional imprisonment.

Escalus: How would you live, Pompey? by being a bawd? What do you think of the trade, Pompey? is it a lawful trade?
Pompey: If the law would allow it, sir.
Escalus: But the law will not allow it, Pompey; ... I advise you, let me not find you before me again upon any complaint whatsoever; no, not for dwelling where you do: if I do, Pompey, I shall beat you to your tent, ... in plain dealing, Pompey, I shall have you whipt: so, for this time, Pompey, fare you well.　　*Measure for Measure*, II, i, 236–65

The duke, on his return, does not condemn Angelo for his strictness, nor Escalus for tempering severity with commonsense and the gift of a second chance. In fact he accepts his work with praise:

> Thanks, good friend Escalus, for thy much goodness:
> V, i, 534

and it is noteworthy that he has never charged either of the deputies to enforce the law without modification. The obligation laid on Angelo is to be as the duke himself, neither more nor less.

> Mortality and mercy in Vienna
> Live in thy tongue and heart:
>> ... your scope is as mine own,
> So to enforce or qualify the laws
> As to your soul seems good. I, i, 44–67

This contains the duke's practical advice to a ruler; even if the more absolute demand could rightly be made, no one in Vienna could fulfil the ideal that the judge's life should always

answer the straitness of his proceeding... wherein if he chance to fail, he hath sentenced himself. III, ii, 270–2

As Pompey—just 'a poor fellow who would live'—explains to Escalus:

Pompey: Does your worship mean to geld and splay all the youth of the city?... Truly, sir, in my poor opinion, they will to't then. If your worship will take order for the drabs and the knaves, you need not to fear the bawds.... If you head and hang all that offend in that way but for ten year together, you'll be glad to give out a commission for more heads: if this law hold in Vienna ten year, I'll rent the fairest house in it after threepence a bay. II, i, 235–55

One of the great beauties of *Measure for Measure* lies in contrast between the world of human society, conditioned by human instincts and economic facts, and the world of the individual in which are possible both sin and its forgiveness. Pompey and Isabella never meet, but it is the tension between their two worlds which makes the polarity of the play. Pompey's exposure of the puritan, the fanatic and all who go about presenting the unpayable demands of the ideal, is as perfect, as clear cut, as irrefutable as Isabella's passionate refusal of all compromise and the duke's repeated demand:

> Be absolute for death; either death or life
> Shall thereby be the sweeter. III, i, 5–6

The structure of the play is raised on the groundwork of Isabella's

values, and it is with her that our sympathies are continually en-
gaged. Nevertheless, the dilemma is not burked. Man must make
on himself the demands he is never able to fulfil. Occasionally the
individual can live on the terms of the ideal; Cordelia could refuse
the ungodly demand of her father as Isabella could that of her
brother. Of such figures are tragedy and poetry made. But their
deeds cannot be imitated in the rough and tumble of daily life by
those who tug and scamble their way between birth and death.

When, after Isabella's farewell to Claudio, the duke becomes the
central figure in the play, his attitude to justice and mercy assumes
a new importance. He condemns nobody to punishment, insisting
merely that wrongs done to other people should be made good.[1]
He does not dispute the desirability of justice, but in spite of his position in the hierarchy of the state, he never dispenses it, and he cannot
therefore be intended to be a direct representative of the Deity.
His contribution to the theme is different and is emphasised by
repetition. Three times he proclaims to a human being that death
is a deserved punishment and in itself a good to be sought. Twice
this is accepted, that is, by Claudio and Angelo, and in each case the
threat of death is withdrawn, the peril circumvented by the duke's
own action. In the third case, Barnardine's, time is given for such
acceptance, so that there is a strong implication that the pattern will
be again repeated. It is of course true that Angelo is not pardoned
for murder, because the duke has seen to it that murder does not
take place, but that does not affect the issue. The individual's plea
for mercy or justice is neither refused nor granted by the state. The
duke works in his own way; his business is to make men fit to die so
that they may become fit to live. And he does just this with Angelo.
When Angelo can say 'I am sorry that such sorrow I procure', he is
safe in Vienna because of what he himself has become, not because
of the women's pleas or the workings of the law.

The Provost makes a very strong proviso that although pardon
should be the word for Claudio, for Barnardine, 'being a murderer,
though he were my brother', death, the direct *quid pro quo*, is the
proper penalty, and as we have seen there are earlier traces that

[1] E.g. Lucio must marry Kate Keepdown.

Shakespeare may have felt sympathy with this attitude. If so his attitude changed. As though determined that the issue should not be fogged, the dramatist brings Barnardine on to the stage at the very climax of Angelo's trial, and he is given the chance of repentance as Claudio and Angelo were, so that the nature of the crime is seen to be irrelevant. *All* have sinned and come short. Society must keep itself in order as best it may. It must seek a middle path and retreat from impossible situations; for it there can be no absolute demands, and since no compromise is possible with death, fallible human beings are well advised to avoid it as a penalty.

This conclusion is forced on the mind by the emergence in *Measure for Measure* of a new 'subject' heard already, in several plays, but in *Measure for Measure* first closely related to the idea of justice. This is the theme of false-seeming, and of man's essential fallibility, since he is unable to judge otherwise than by appearances. Here is the thread which we follow into the next plays. After *Measure for Measure* Shakespeare ceases to concern himself deeply with the problem of justice and mercy in the state. He turns from man's relation to his prince and his fellow-man to his relations with his God and those to whom he is bound by the passions of love and hatred, rather than by social propinquity. The old dilemma is treated once more, however, and the tone leaves no doubt that the attitude, accepted even by Portia in *The Merchant of Venice* but finally refuted in *Measure for Measure*, is being held up to obloquy.

In *Timon of Athens*, Alcibiades appeals to the Senate for a reprieve for a friend condemned to death for duelling, a brave soldier whose services plead for him. The leading Senator voices in noble rhetoric the old principle that the state should give 'naught but justice', and he gives the old reason—the protection of the commonwealth.

> *First Senator*:   the fault's
> Bloody; 'tis necessary he should die:
> Nothing emboldens sin so much as mercy....
> *Alcibiades*: I am an humble suitor to your virtues;
> For pity is a virtue of the law,...
>   O my lords,
> As you are great, be pitifully good:...

> To kill, I grant, is sin's extremest gust;
> But, in defence, by mercy, 'tis most just....
> *First Senator*: We are for law; he dies; urge it no more,
> On height of our displeasure; friend or brother,
> He forfeits his own blood that spills another.   III, v, 1–88

It all sounds well enough until we remember who the senators are
—men whose role in the play is to pay nothing to true desert, or
rather to reward it with ignominy, and to exploit the generosity
of others to gain their own ends. We are clearly invited to despise
them in our hearts, as Timon does:

> *Timon*:   slaves and fools,
> Pluck the grave wrinkled senate from the bench,
> And minister in their steads!   IV, i, 4–6

Such men are as unfitted as Angelo to dispense the law. Alcibiades
is a swashbuckling cut-throat, but we sympathise with him more
than with his stony adversaries.

> *Alcibiades*: Must it be so? it must not be. My lords,
> I do beseech you, know me.
> *Second Senator*:   How!
> *Alcibiades*: Call me to your remembrances.
> *Third Senator*:   What!
> *Alcibiades*: I cannot think but your age has forgot me;
> It could not else be, I should prove so base,
> To sue, and be denied such common grace;
> My wounds ache at you.   III, v, 89–95

Justice here, as in Venice, upholds the legal bonds and is concerned
with profit and loss only.

> *Alcibiades*:   I have kept back their foes,
> While they have told their money and let out
> Their coin upon large interest, I myself
> Rich only in large hurts.   III, v, 106–9

Whatever principles the Senate of Athens upholds in this play, it
does no more than hold them up to ridicule. If this is justice it is no
longer adequate to the needs of the people. But Shakespeare's
imagination, as we have seen, was ceasing to be actively involved

with the relationship of rulers with the ruled, and in the next plays to be considered the violence of his concern with justice and mercy finds expression in the lives of his greatest tragic individuals.

CHAPTER IV

JUSTICE, MERCY AND FALSE-SEEMING

Miracle and Morality Plays; *Measure for Measure*;
The Merchant of Venice; *Much Ado about Nothing*; *Hamlet*;
Coriolanus; *Julius Caesar*; *Othello*

After *Measure for Measure*, although a trial may still appear as a muted theme in situation, as when Lear arraigns Goneril and Regan,[1] or in imagery, as when Macbeth imagines even-handed justice commending his poisoned chalice to his own lips,[2] Shakespeare puts aside the simple symbolism so effective in the long development of the *Débat du Paradis* and illuminates man's concern with justice and mercy by other means. It appears to be significant that he abandons the structure so strongly associated with the religious drama at the very moment when his own plays become most numinous in quality. The Christian tradition in which his thought is rooted is centred in the polarity between fear and love. These are the values that the 'machiavel', Richard, explicitly denies:

I, that have neither pity, love, nor fear,

3 Henry VI, v, vi, 68

and which Shakespeare never abandons. The necessary fear of evil and of its just punishment is as genuine in *The Tempest* as in *Richard III* and only less powerful than the love which finally transcends it. Nevertheless, the melting of the old imagery in the white heat of the later tragedies is no coincidence, for it can be shown that Shakespeare finally indicates a resolution of the paradox of Justice and Mercy in non-dogmatic terms. Before this is discussed, however, it is necessary to consider the subordinate but relevant theme of false-seeming and its power to deceive and destroy.

In the *Ludus Coventriae*, Misericordia, in her plea for man, said to her sister Justicia:

[1] *King Lear*, III, vi.   [2] *Macbeth*, I, vii.

Ye must consider the frailness of mankind;
Learn and ye list, this is God's love;

Parliament of Heaven, ll. 110–11

Here man's natural frailty is directly related to his need for God's mercy, and the frailty is nowhere more evident than in his inability to penetrate below appearance.[1] Thus we approach the theme of false-seeming which for a time succeeds the debate between Justice and Mercy as a determining pattern in Shakespeare's work. This theme also had made its first stage appearance in the miracle plays where it was particularly associated with Lucifer, that 'outward sainted' spirit whose

filth within being cast, he would appear
A pond as deep as hell.

Measure for Measure, III, i, 93–4

In the York play of *The Creation*, he cries:

The form of all fairness upon me is fast...
The beams of my brightness are built with the best.
My showing is shimmering and shining.

His deceptive beauty even after his fall is sometimes stressed as it is in the *Ludus Coventriae* version of the temptation of Eve.

Eve to Adam: A fair angel thus said me to,
'To eat that apple, take never no dread'...

Fall of Man, ll. 238–9

Eve to God: Lord when thou wentest forth from this place
A worm with an angel's face
He hyeth us to be full of grace
The fruit if that we eate.
I did his bidding. Alas Alas.
Now we be bounden in death's las[2]
I suppose it was Sathanas   ll. 302 ff.

There is an ironic little scene in the Chester cycle based on a different kind of disguise, which also found its way into Shakespeare's

---

[1] The inability of man to penetrate the false-seeming of evil is an important element in the pleading of Misericorde in the *Mistere du Viel Testament* but this thought is not developed forcibly in the English versions of the Debate.
[2] Snare.

plays. In the massacre at Bethlehem the soldiers kill a child who is Herod's own son put out to nurse to a woman in the village. She rushes to Herod with her complaint.

> *Secunda Mulier*: Loe lord, loke and see!
> The child that thou took to me,
> Men of thine owne meny
> Have slayn it, . . .
> *Herod*: He was right sicker in silk aray,
> In gould and pirrye that was so gay
> They might well know by his aray
> He was a kinges son.   *Slaying of the Innocents*, ll. 393 ff.

This is a false prince, but his role is not that of a hypocrite but of a martyr. He is slain so that the true prince may escape, even as, with a double irony, Douglas slays Blount, disguised in a king's coat so that a false king's life is saved.

It is in the moralities, however, that false-seeming becomes an important motif; so much so that it is partly the necessity of re-membering which Vice is disguised under the name of which Virtue that makes some of them laborious reading. It must be remembered that when they were acted—as they were meant to be —the identity of the vices would always be clear. Disguise appears to have gone no further in most cases than a change of name; in *Respublica*, for example, Avarice takes on the name of Policy; Insolence of Authority, Adulation of Honesty and Oppression of Reformation.

In Sir David Lindsay's *Satire of the Three Estates* (1540),[1] however, real dramatic use is made of the disguising of the Vices, which is treated as high comedy. Flattery suggests their plan:

> We must turn our clothes and change our styles.

This they quickly do, Deceit using a monk's gown. They next decide to change their names also and go through a mock ceremony of baptism, christening each other in turn.

> *Falsehood*: I wot not how to call mysel'!
> *Deceit*: But yet once name the bairn's name!

---

[1] *Satire of the Three Estates*, ed. by T. Guthrie.

I

> *Falsehood*: Discretion, Discretion in God's name!...

Flattery's turn comes next:

> *Flattery*: Brother Deceit come baptise me!
> *Deceit*: Then sit down lowly on thy knee!
> *Flattery*: Now brother name the bairn's name.
> *Deceit*: Devotion in the Devil's name.
> *Flattery*: The deil receive thee, lurdan loon!
> Thou has wet all my new shaven crown!

When the king asks them their names Falsehood forgets his new one.

> *Falsehood*: Marry, sir, they call me—what call they me?
> (*Aside*) I wot not well, but if I be!
> *King*: Can you not tell me what is your name?
> *Falsehood*: I knew it when I came from home!...
> *Deceit*: (*Aside*) Sapience, thou serves to bear a plate!...
> *Flattery*: (*To the King*) Sir, if you please to let me say,
> That same is Sapientia!
> *Falsehood*: That same it is, by St Michael!
> *King*: Why could thou not tell it thysel?

At the judgment the sinners are all stripped of their disguises and one is a prioress who has earlier refused shelter to Lady Chastity.

> *First Sergeant*: Come on my lady Prioress,
> We shall learn you to dance.

He obviously must tear off her habit here and show a gay dress underneath it for the second sergeant exclaims:

> Now brother, by the Mass
> By my judgment I think
> This holy Prioress
> Has turned a cow clink!

The Prioress is given a defence, however, which makes her after all into a sympathetic character:

> I give my friends my malison
> That me compelled to be a nun
> And would not let me marry!...

> But I shall do the best I can,
> And marry some good honest man,
> And brew good ale in tun!
>
> Marriage, by my opinion,
> Is a better religion
>   Than to be friar or nun!

It is not many stage hypocrites who are let off so pleasantly!

Disguise appears in a form closer to Shakespeare's manner in the chronicle play of *John, King of England*[1] whose author, John Bale, makes effective use of this Morality convention. In Act I, for example, there is the stage direction: 'Usurped Power shall dress for the Pope; Private Wealth for a Cardinal; and Sedition for a Monk.' Shortly afterwards these three abstractions, their faces still recognisable of course, appear as Innocent III, Cardinal Pandulph and Stephen Langton and proceed to play out the historical events of John's reign as they were interpreted by a fighting Lutheran pastor with a considerable gift of dramatic vituperation.

Shakespeare was fascinated by the potentialities of disguise; masked revellers and maidens dressed as boys jostle their way through many of the gayest comedies, and an animal's head may all unwittingly betray the ass beneath the skin. But it is Ben Jonson who directly inherits from Sir David Lindsay and his anonymous predecessors in the world of satire. When 'the smiler with the knife beneath the cloak' presents a dangerous threat to goodness, Shakespeare returns to the older miracle tradition, and at his hands the false friend, the subtle villain, the charming 'machiavel' are in the major tragedies stripped of their coverings amid tears, not laughter.

The conflict of Justice and Mercy is still central in *Measure for Measure* but it is complicated in that play by the growing strength of a counter-subject.

> *Isabella:*   Seeming, seeming!
> I will proclaim thee, Angelo; look for't:
> Sign me a present pardon for my brother,

---

[1] *Dramatic Writings of John Bale.* E.E.D.S., ed. by J. S. Farmer.

Or with an out-stretch'd throat I'll tell the world aloud
What man thou art.
Angelo: Who will believe thee, Isabel?
Measure for Measure, II, iv, 150–4

In the first half of Act v the dramatic tension depends as much on Isabella's inability to make the truth believed as upon her demand for justice.

Isabella: O prince, I conjure thee,...
                          Make not impossible
That which but seems unlike: 'tis not impossible
But one, the wicked'st caitiff on the ground,
May seem as shy, as grave, as just, as absolute
As Angelo; even so may Angelo
In all his dressings, characts, titles, forms,
Be an arch-villain....   v, i, 48–57

The structure of *Measure for Measure* is based on the ways in which the duke does in fact fulfil Isabella's plea:

                          let your reason serve
To make the truth appear where it seems hid,
And hide the false seems true.   v, i, 65–7

As the theme of Justice *versus* Mercy, so that of false-seeming finds its way into Shakespeare's earliest comedy. It is not merely that the plot of *The Comedy of Errors* turns on the impossibility of distinguishing between identical twins: perhaps ' 'twould be to consider too-curiously to consider so', though it is not without interest to find Shakespeare's imagination captivated so early by just such a story. Luciana's words to the Antipholus whom she wrongly believes to be her erring brother-in-law, however, although clearly written in the vein of lightest comedy, have yet a genuine ring of a morality play about them:

Muffle your false love with some show of blindness:...
Look sweet, speak fair, become disloyalty;
   Apparel vice like virtue's harbinger;
Bear a fair presence, though your heart be tainted;
   Teach sin the carriage of a holy saint;
Be secret-false.   III, ii, 8–15

The interest persists through the early comedies: *A Midsummer-Night's Dream* turns on the failure of the eye to perceive truly, and the inability to penetrate disguise in *Love's Labour's Lost* is not entirely a matter of stage convention. In *Much Ado about Nothing*, Borachio claims: 'I have deceived even your very eyes', and Claudio's sin, slight though its treatment, is of the same nature as Othello's. The helplessness of the lovers, betrayed by the lying image of Borachio at Hero's window, has a touch of true tragic quality. Their dilemma is inescapable and hence fearful as well as pitiable.[1]

> *Claudio*: Give not this rotten orange to your friend;
> She's but the sign and semblance of her honour...
> Out on thee! Seeming![2]...
> But fare thee well, most foul, most fair! farewell.
> Thou pure impiety and impious purity!
> For thee I'll lock up all the gates of love,
> And on my eyelids shall conjecture hang,
> To turn all beauty into thoughts of harm,
> And never shall it more be gracious.   IV, i, 33–108

In *The Merchant of Venice* false-seeming had already been associated with a story of Justice and Mercy, but it appears a fortuitous juxtaposition without particular significance. In view of the later development, however, it is of interest to notice the two themes lying, as it were, parallel in Shakespeare's mind before their intrinsic interdependence became clear to his imagination.

'Who chooseth me shall gain what many men desire', says Morocco, only to learn that 'all that glisters is not gold'. 'I will assume desert', says Arragon, and discovers that beneath his princely panoply he is 'a blinking idiot'. In Belmont, however, the threat of false-seeming to goodness is not serious, for love (although not *fancy* which by its very nature must be 'engender'd in the eyes') is not deceived by it.

> *Bassanio*: So may the outward shows be least themselves:

---

[1] Any sensitive stage production puts this beyond doubt.

[2] Cf. 'Out on thee seeming', Folio. Sometimes amended to 'Out on the seeming'. A direct address to Hero as indicated by F. seems the strongest interpretation.

The world is still deceived with ornament.
    ... Therefore, thou gaudy gold,
Hard food for Midas, I will none of thee;
Nor none of thee, thou pale and common drudge
'Tween man and man; but thou, thou meagre lead,
Which rather threatenest than dost promise aught,
Thy paleness moves me more than eloquence;
And here choose I; joy be the consequence!

Merchant of Venice, III, ii, 73–107

It is however in *Hamlet* and *Othello* that the twin themes of justice and false-seeming find their greatest expression. Hamlet starts boldly:

Seems, madam! nay, it is; I know not 'seems'.

Hamlet, I, ii, 76

He is confident that he can always see through appearances to reality, as clearly as he does when he probes the shallowness of his mother's grief:

            or ere those shoes were old
With which she follow'd my poor father's body,
Like Niobe, all tears:...
She married.   I, ii, 147–56

Yet after his task is laid upon him, when clarity of vision becomes all-important, he loses confidence in his own power of insight:

            The spirit that I have seen
May be the devil; and the devil hath power
To assume a pleasing shape; yea, and perhaps
Out of my weakness and my melancholy,
As he is very potent in such spirits,
Abuses me to damn me.   II, ii, 627–32

But if the devil can take a pleasing shape, a loved father may take a horrific one, so Hamlet must remain on the alert to pierce that which

    ... will but skin and film the ulcerous place
While rank corruption, mining all within,
Infects unseen.   III, iv, 147–9

He even becomes unsure of his own nature and can believe in his courage no more than in his mother's grief or Ophelia's chastity:

> Am I a coward?
> Who calls me villain? breaks my pate across?...
> 'Swounds, I should take it! for it cannot be
> But I am pigeon-liver'd.   II, ii, 598–605

With the self-assurance which follows on the success of the Mouse-Trap and the return from the sea voyage, Hamlet develops a new power to look below life's surfaces without flinching. He can now meditate quietly on Yorick's skull or Alexander's dust and penetrate Laertes' over-dressed, vociferous grief as confidently as once, clad in the garments of true mourning, he had defied Gertrude to find the slightest falsity beneath them.

> I am very sorry, good Horatio,
> That to Laertes I forgot myself;...
> But, sure, the bravery of his grief did put me
> Into a towering passion.   V, ii, 75–9

At last, sure of the truth that the king is to blame, he can achieve his task, but he cannot distinguish between a clean and a poisoned rapier, for human eyes are not equipped to do so even though a man's life depend on the knowledge.

The vision of Hamlet as a righteous 'justicer' because, not in spite, of the delays which the necessity of penetrating below the multiple false-seemings of life impose, is clarified by the structure of the play, which places beside him the figures of two other men who attempt to re-establish their honour by avenging the death of a father. Laertes does fulfil Hamlet's own early promise: he sweeps to his revenge 'with wings as swift as meditation or the thoughts of love'. Claudius may well demand of him:

> is't writ in your revenge,
> That, swoopstake, you will draw both friend and foe,
> Winner and loser?

and to Laertes' disclaimer, 'none but his enemies', the king replies with the essential question:

> Will you know them then?   IV, v, 141–4

Laertes becomes Claudius' stooge so easily because he accepts without question that the true enemy is the one pointed out to him. He does not consider that a man may smile and be a villain, or that the devil may assume a disguise; he is aware of no need for delay or question.

> I'll not be juggled with:
> To hell, allegiance! vows, to the blackest devil!
> Conscience and grace, to the profoundest pit!
> I dare damnation.   IV, v, 130–3

He is very easily juggled with none the less, and the daring of damnation—the very thing that Hamlet will not do—leads him to kill another man's enemy, in a 'brother's wager' played with an unbated poisoned rapier and begun with the words:

> I do receive your offer'd love like love,
> And will not wrong it.   v, ii, 262–3

But in spite of his treachery Shakespeare appears to have meant him to escape the damnation which he so glibly dared since, unlike Claudius, he seizes the chance offered him to repent and make what amends he can.

> *Laertes*: The treacherous instrument is in thy hand,
> Unbated and envenom'd:...
> I can no more; the king, the king's to blame....
> Exchange forgiveness with me, noble Hamlet:
> Mine and my father's death come not upon thee,
> Nor thine on me.   v, ii, 327–42

Hamlet is right to see in Laertes' cause the portraiture of his own, but the image is on a negative; the sides and colours are reversed. Laertes does exactly what Hamlet refuses to do—he attempts to base justice on appearances—and he proves that Hamlet was right to await the knowledge and the opportunity which delay brought him. It is Hamlet's hesitation joined to his uncle's deviousness which perfect the old pattern of the 'revenge' play. In *Hamlet* Shakespeare has written a play in which all the riches of his psychological insight are used to convey with subtlety and convincing realism the same simple message as did *The Spanish Tragedy*:[1]

---

[1] Cf. above, pp. 87 ff.

> The sickle comes not till the corn be ripe; II, vi, 9

or, in Hamlet's words:

> There's a divinity that shapes our ends,
> Rough-hew them how we will… *Hamlet*, v, ii, 110–11

For men, 'the readiness is all'; they must prepare themselves to be, in Malcolm's words, the 'instruments' of the powers above.

The relationship between Hamlet and Fortinbras is as close as that between Hamlet and Laertes, but it is deeply equivocal. Fortinbras is apparently both a loyal and courageous son. He has sharked up 'a list of lawless resolutes' with which he may avenge on Denmark the death of his father and the loss of a part of his kingdom; he submits, however, to the pressure put upon him by his uncle and turns his forces against Poland. The episode is lightly sketched in, but Fortinbras' attack is definitely unprovoked and made for his personal ends. It is in fact closely parallel to Henry V's attack on France, which took place on the advice of a father not unlike the usurper Claudius, in order to 'busy giddy minds with foreign quarrels' (*2 Henry IV*, IV, v, 214-15). This is the expedition which Hamlet passes on his way to England, and by the sight of which he is stimulated to vow afresh his ultimate revenge. The reason for the vow is not necessarily approval of Fortinbras' action, however, for the decision is worded with considerable ambiguity:

> Rightly to be great
> Is not to stir without great argument,
> But greatly to find quarrel in a straw
> When honour's at the stake. How stand I then,
> That have a father kill'd, a mother stain'd,
> Excitements of my reason and my blood,
> And let all sleep? IV, iv, 53–9

Hamlet is quite sure that his own honour is at the stake; as for the honour of Fortinbras, on it he makes no comment. Like that of the more famous King Henry whom he so resembles, the action of Fortinbras was doubtless approved by the vulgar, but the judicious may well have seen cause to grieve, even if their company included, in this case, only the playwright himself. If it be objected that an unfavourable interpretation of Fortinbras is impermissible because when he finally receives Hamlet's dying voice for the succession in Denmark and pays the last honours to the dead prince, it should be remembered that Shakespeare does not always show the new era bringing with it much hope of better things. It is, after all, Octavius Caesar, who succeeds Mark Antony.[1] Fortinbras is thus, like Laertes, designed as an image of Hamlet in reverse. His revenge is not correctly aimed. Once more Hamlet's delay is vindicated, for through it the divine justice is finally achieved.[2]

A later play on vengeance throws the nature of Hamlet's conduct into still clearer relief. In *Coriolanus* we watch an action which is apparently conceived by its perpetrator as just punishment and yet is palpably wrong. Coriolanus' march on Rome is a direct result of the Roman people's action; as they brewed so are they to drink. Yet the words in which he puts his proposition to Aufidius show clearly that it is an infamous one, that it is designed to ensure a terrible vengeance for a purely personal injury and that in exacting it Coriolanus is acting diabolically:

> speed thee straight,
> And make my misery serve thy turn:...
> for I will fight
> Against my canker'd country with the spleen
> Of all the under fiends.   IV, V, 93–8

Coriolanus is not, like Hamlet, the scourge and minister of heaven; he works with the cruelty and arrogance of a devil and arrogates to himself the right to be judge and executioner in his own cause. When Volumnia pleads with him she is striving not, like Isabella, to voice the Divine Mercy and find a way of applying it to human affairs but simply to prevent a blind retaliation, exacted

---

[1] See pp. 67–8 and 174–5.

[2] Professor H. Levin has recently suggested, in *The Question of Hamlet* (1959), that Fortinbras is the acceptable successor because he alone of the play's avengers is not guilty of murder. This is an attractive idea, but Shakespeare's treatment of the 'saviour' princes does not necessarily show approval of them, and the point is not therefore conclusive. See below, p. 172.

'swoop-stake' on friend and foe. She succeeds:

> O my mother, mother!
> You have won a happy victory to Rome;
> But, for your son,—believe it, O, believe it,
> Most dangerously you have with him prevail'd.

v, iii, 185–8

Coriolanus, like Macbeth, knew that:

> I am in blood
> Stepp'd in so far that, should I wade no more,
> Returning were as tedious as go o'er.

Macbeth, III, iv, 136–8

Unlike Macbeth, he does attempt to return, but he is drowned before he reaches the hither bank. Our sympathy goes out to him in his death, and Shakespeare must have intended this to be so, for he puts the seal of his approval on Coriolanus' retreat from Rome by giving him a farewell almost as moving as Hamlet's own:

> *Aufidius*:   My rage is gone;
> And I am struck with sorrow. Take him up.
> Help, three o' the chiefest soldiers; I'll be one.
> Beat thou the drum, that it speak mournfully:
> Trail your steel pikes. Though in this city he
> Hath widow'd and unchilded many a one,
> Which to this hour bewail the injury,
> Yet he shall have a noble memory.
> Assist.   v, vi, 148–56

Nevertheless, Coriolanus is the direct opposite of Hamlet. His vengeance is unrelated to justice. He is 'not of stronger earth than others', but he perceives the truth too late for it to save him.

It is in the light of this emphasis on the necessity of the clear vision that the central significance of *Julius Caesar* must be assessed. The role and character of Brutus become clear once he is presented as a man of double vision, one who is unaware of reality and can assess correctly neither persons nor situations, so that in attempting to do so he may unwittingly contradict his own most cherished principles. His opposition to the proposed 'liquidation' of Antony is based on moral principles:

Cassius: his means,
If he improve them, may well stretch so far
As to annoy us all; which to prevent,
Let Antony and Caesar fall together.
Brutus: Our course will seem too bloody, Caius Cassius...
Let us be sacrificers, but not butchers, Caius.   II, i, 158–66

Yet prevention is the very justification he has already used to excuse
his own earlier decision when, after he has reflected that the upward
climber is likely to destroy the ladder by which he has ascended, he
adds:

So Caesar may.
Then, lest he may, prevent.   II, i, 27–8

For a moment he sees the conspirators for what they are. He calls
them the *faction*—a word of ill sound to Elizabethan ears—and in
his soliloquy uses concerning them imagery similar to that of
Worcester's speech to the rebels:[1]

O conspiracy...
Where wilt thou find a cavern dark enough
To mask thy monstrous visage?   II, i, 77–81

But he goes on deliberately to invoke that 'false-seeming' which he
hates and which is so much more effective a covering than darkness.

Seek none, conspiracy;
Hide it in smiles and affability:
For if thou path,[2] thy native semblance on,
Not Erebus itself were dim enough
To hide thee from prevention.   II, i, 81–5

Julius Caesar is a tragedy not of human wickedness but of human
inadequacy. Caesar is deaf and childless; his faults are the infantile
ones of vanity, obstinacy, blindness to flattery. The 'lean and
hungry' Cassius has always been short-sighted; his friend calls him
'waspish' and 'a slight man', and he himself apologises for his hot
temper as womanish. In spite of this he mocks his great enemy for

---

[1] See above, p. 29.   [2] Make your way.

crying out 'like a sick girl', and perhaps a man who could himself have swum the Tiber more easily would not have jibed at Caesar so bitterly for failing to do so. Brutus misjudges in turn Cassius, Portia (her behaviour before the assassination shows that it was indeed risky to trust her with such weighty secrets), Mark Antony and the Roman populace, as well as the friends whom he hoped would help him to escape from life. Perhaps he misjudged Caesar too; he certainly 'but slenderly knew himself', and he could not put into practice the stern philosophy he believed he held. *Julius Caesar* is a play concerning clouded vision; it belongs not to the world of the History Plays or of the Luciferian tragedies, but to the world of *Othello*, where 'ignorant armies clash by night', and men are not equipped to penetrate to that truth on a knowledge of which their salvation depends. Each of the chief characters might well admit in Cassius' simple words: 'My sight was ever thick' (v, iii, 21).

In *Othello* man's salvation again depends on his ability to distinguish truth from false-seeming, and this theme is linked again with that of justice. Both Othello and Desdemona believe they are able to see truth beneath its disguise, but the primary cause of Othello's downfall is not his jealousy but his spiritual blindness. He is right when he says he was not easily jealous but was 'perplexed in the extreme'. In his perplexity he makes a twofold mistake: Iago, in spite of a rough, blunt, unpleasing exterior, he judges to be good, and Desdemona he judges to be a devil behind a mask of angelic beauty. Iago put up an excellent case, and against it Othello had no defence. He was not equipped to understand 'a super subtle Venetian' nor know whether or not her

> ...best conscience
> Is not to leave't undone, but keep't unknown.   III, iii, 203-4

But the difficulty was more profound than any problems set either by Othello's temperament or by his ignorance of Italian society. There is *no rational answer* to Iago's proposition that love is a lust of the blood and a permission of the will; there are *no reasons* to be found for loyalty. Man's only safety is to recognise goodness and to trust it, and the tragic core of the play is that while he has an absolute need to apprehend spiritual truths he is without the faculties necessary to do so with certainty.[1]

In his spiritual blindness Othello indulges in the grotesque parody of justice in which he condemns Desdemona for adultery and executes her upon her wedding sheets.

Iago: Strangle her in her bed, even the bed she hath contaminated.
Othello: Good, good: the justice of it pleases: very good.   IV, i, 220–2

He sees himself as heaven's justicer: 'it is the cause',[2] and he uses the old argument for retributive justice—its social usefulness:

> Yet she must die, else she'll betray more men.   v, ii, 6

We remember Angelo's cold response to Isabella:

> I show it [pity] most of all when I show justice,
> For then I pity those I do not know,
> Which a dismiss'd offence would after gall.
>
> *Measure for Measure*, II, ii, 100–2

For a moment Othello is on the very verge of the truth:

> Ah, balmy breath, that dost almost persuade
> Justice to break her sword!   v, ii, 16–17

But the momentary vision passes, and he succumbs again, blinded by the terrible illusion of his own right to judge, an illusion so complete that he sees himself acting as the Christian's God would act:

> this sorrow's heavenly;
> It strikes where it doth love.   v, ii, 21–2

In fact Othello has thrown over his Christianity along with his faith in Desdemona's goodness.

> If she be false, O, then heaven mocks itself!   III, iii, 278

was a true forecast of the working of his mind. When he doubted her he forgot his baptism and returned to the values of an older way of life, taught him by the mother who bequeathed her beliefs as well as her magic handkerchief to her child. Once caught in the current

---

[1] Since this was written the author has read with great pleasure Professor Heilman's detailed exposition of a similar point of view in *Magic in the Web: Action and Language in Othello*, 1956.

[2] I.e. the case brought for judgment.

of primitive emotions he never questions the righteousness of that
'kind of wild justice' his forebears would have wreaked:

> O, that the slave had forty thousand lives!
> One is too poor, too weak for my revenge.   III, iii, 442–3

Only when his faith in Desdemona has been restored to him does
he remember his Christianity, and then it brings him the knowledge of his own damnation.

> Oh, ill-starr'd wench!
> Pale as thy smock! when we shall meet at compt,
> This look of thine will hurl my soul from heaven,
> And fiends will snatch at it.   v, ii, 272–5

There is a horrifying ambiguity about Desdemona's judgment of
Othello. 'I saw Othello's visage in his mind', she says, with a perfect confidence that the black face belies the purity of the mind
which it hides—an opinion which at the time all but Brabantio
share. But at the end when we watch him, a wife-murderer, en-
slaved by a demi-devil, asking for the damnation he believed he
deserved and seeking it in the final despair of suicide, we may
wonder if she were not mistaken.[1] Othello asks that he should not
be judged by his appearance: he claims:

> My parts, my title and my perfect soul
> Shall manifest me rightly.   I, ii, 31–2

He, no more than Angelo, however, knew what manner of man he
was, and unlike Angelo he never achieves more than a partial self-
knowledge. To the end he covers the full horror of his failure from
his own eyes, calling himself, 'an honourable murderer, if you
will'. Angelo would not have used of his sin that falsely gleaming
adjective. Othello understands the fruits of his sin rather than the
sin itself. He knows that he has thrown his pearl away and that he
deserves death; like Angelo he desires it, but unlike Angelo he
never submits to the 'power divine', which could have saved him.[2]

---

[1] Cf.   Duncan: There's no art
               To find the mind's construction in the face.   Macbeth, I, iv, 11–12
[2] It is of considerable interest that a recent interpretation of the play based on a naturalistic psychological analysis reaches a similar conclusion. Othello 'has discovered his mistake,
but there is no tragic self-discovery' (F. R. Leavis, The Common Pursuit, p. 150).

The Duke of Venice had offered Brabantio the satisfaction of 'justice' with the words:

> ...the bloody book of law
> You shall yourself read in the bitter letter.   I, iii, 67-8

Othello himself can see no further and do no better than this. We look back to that blessed world of Vienna where men and women were saved from the seemingly irrevocable penalties of their own idiocy by a wisdom which accepted the limitations of human eyesight and was willing to allow time for changes of heart rather than impose a final penalty. As Othello had arrogated to himself the right to deal out 'justice' to Desdemona, so he assumes the right to do what he considers to be justice on himself. Even when he dies, therefore, he is still occupying the usurped throne of the only true Judge. When Othello's vision is partially cleansed by suffering he sees his sin, but he does not see its remedy. No more than Macbeth can he face the humiliation of trial and punishment, and the very virtue by which he recognises the blackness of his trespass leads him into the further sin of despair. 'Is not my soul my own?' cried Dr Faustus, and the Christian answer is certainly 'No'. The final denial of life is in reality not murder but self-murder, and moreover the suicide may die in a way that gives him no chance to repent of his last and therefore truly mortal sin. Shakespeare is at pains to emphasise the swiftness of Othello's death. This most famous of dramatic surprises is no mere *coup de théâtre*; it is essential to the imaginative situation that Othello die suddenly though deliberately, without time for repentance.

The obliquity of the distorted image exacts at last the price not merely of bodily but of spiritual death. Desdemona dies, but her last words, expressing the mercy which forgives and strives to save, leave her for ever an image of life:

> *Desdemona*: A guiltless death I die.
> *Emilia*: O, who hath done this deed?
> *Desdemona*: Nobody; I myself. Farewell:
>   Commend me to my kind lord: O, farewell!   v, ii, 122-5

Othello's death on the other hand represents absolute loss, as Macbeth's does, and it is the direct result of his inability to penetrate the false-seeming of Iago. It will be shown later that *Othello* bridges the thought of the tragedies and that of the romances, and it seems at least possible that his contemplation of Othello's end marked a turning-point in the growth of Shakespeare's imaginative vision. The social-religious thought of his time marked Othello, the unrepentant suicide, inevitably for damnation. As Shakespeare has developed the character this is a situation which may well have appeared to him unendurable, an emotional and intellectual *impasse* from which he could find an exit only by breaking out from the fabric of contemporary thought, and such a breaking out does in fact take place in the last plays.

In *Antony and Cleopatra* Shakespeare perhaps gives the screw one further turn, for Antony in a flash of unusual insight realises that it is a man's own previous actions which blind him. Like the earlier moralists, he sees in this the hidden hand of a divine Justice:

> But when we in our viciousness grow hard—
> O misery on't!—the wise gods seel our eyes;
> In our own filth drop our clear judgements; make us
> Adore our errors; laugh at's, while we strut
> To our confusion. III, xiii, 110–14

Whether Othello blinds himself or whether he is born blind, however, his story remains as grim a vision of *la condition humaine* as Shakespeare ever painted, and only the love of Desdemona redeems it from a despair as black as Othello's own. Any assertion of the absolute inability of man to distinguish between good and evil would be a denial of the Christian belief in man's responsibility to God and his neighbour, a denial also of the impression given by the *corpus* of Shakespeare's own work. The twin dangers of which we have already heard in the pleading of Mercy in *The Parliament of Heaven*—that man was cleverly tempted and that he was by nature frail and easily deceived—are peculiarly strong in the two plays which end with the damnation of their hero, and Macbeth, although his sight is so much more penetrating than Othello's, is also troubled by the ambiguity of appearances: he misinterprets all the witches' 'sights' and his first words are:

So foul and fair a day I have not seen,[1]   I, iii, 38

Whether the figures of Iago and of the witches are apprehended as imaging supernatural forces which are external to man or evil within his own personality will depend primarily on the 'climate of opinion' in which the plays are read or seen. Shakespeare was apparently able to share both attitudes of mind, for the plays permit both. The conflict between Othello and Iago has been interpreted as lying between two sides of one schizoid personality,[2] whereas the original audience would have been more inclined, with Othello, to seek for the ensign's cloven hoof [3] and certainly for the most part believed that the witches served a power quite independent of Macbeth. Nevertheless, the difference in the imaginative impact of the two interpretations is less than might have been expected. What is essential is that the dramatic figures presenting the situation should not be thought of as abnormal or psychopathic, for the evil which destroys them is conceived as an inevitable danger, a universal threat to the normal man which he fails to resist only at his peril.

Furthermore, in spite of every intrinsic weakness and external pressure, there is no final sense of compulsion about the course Othello and Macbeth both follow to their own undoing; time and occasion for repentance and salvation are offered to each and deliberately refused. Shakespeare at this time appears to offer only one possible aid to man in his dilemma, and this is the love of another human being: Othello and Macbeth, both by their own faults and the misfortunes of chance, face their final struggle *alone*. King Lear does not, and for him the outcome is significantly different.

---

[1] Cf. Claudio, above, p. 125.
[2] J. I. M. Stewart, *Character and Motive in Shakespeare*.
[3] 'I look down towards his feet; but that's a fable' (v, ii, 285).

CHAPTER V

PARDON AND PUNISHMENT

Titus Andronicus; *Henry VI*; *King Lear*; *Timon of Athens*

King Lear, in which Shakespeare takes up and transcends the various images of justice, mercy and false-seeming which he had previously created, and fuses them into a whole of new and terrible beauty, has two early precursors of considerable interest. *Titus Andronicus*, offers an unusually vivid example of the long incubation which a thought may undergo in a poet's mind. Titus, like Lear, is an old man driven mad by the loss of his all, yet retaining in madness a clear knowledge of his own wrongs and of their perpetrators. Like Lear he has begun his own undoing by driving from him his child, Mutius, whom he unjustly kills and by trusting in the specious words of his enemies to whom he surrenders the realm of which he could have been chosen emperor. Having given them everything he is driven to madness, finally dying himself and killing the beautiful and virtuous daughter whom he loves.

Lastly, as Lear does, Titus seeks from heaven the justice denied him on earth. In a grotesque but tragic scene he addresses petitions to the gods, sending to Pluto by messenger and dispatching the other petitions by shooting them skyward on arrows. The first message is to Pluto.

> Tell him, it is for justice and for aid,
> And that it comes from old Andronicus.[1]   IV, III, 15–16

Publius brings answer:

>   Pluto sends you word,
> If you will have Revenge from hell, you shall:
> Marry, for Justice, she is so employ'd,
> He thinks, with Jove in heaven, or somewhere else,
> So that perforce you must needs stay a time.   IV, iii, 37–41

[1] Cf. *King Lear*, II, iv, 192–5. See below, pp. 147–8.

But Titus holds to his faith in heaven's justice.

> And, sith there's no justice in earth nor hell,
> We will solicit heaven and move the gods
> To send down Justice for to wreak our wrongs.
>
> IV, iii, 49–51

The arrows are sent off by his old brother, a prototype of Kent, and three loyal friends who humour him in his madness, as Lear is humoured by Edgar and the fool. These messages finally reach the ears of the emperor. Saturninus, unlike the evil characters in *King Lear*, still thinks it worth while to use the 'value' words of the old order to cloak his unscrupulous pursuit of his private ends. He protests that:

> nought hath pass'd,
> But even with law, against the wilful sons
> Of old Andronicus....
> What's this but libelling against the senate,
> And blazoning our injustice every where?
> A goodly humour, is it not, my lords?
> As who would say, in Rome no justice were.   IV, iv, 7–20

He is, however, extraordinarily like Goneril and Regan in the down-to-earth sweet reasonableness of his most callous statements:

> And what an if
> His sorrows have so overwhelm'd his wits,
> Shall we be thus afflicted in his wreaks,
> His fits, his frenzy, and his bitterness?
> And now he writes to heaven for his redress:...
> Sweet scrolls to fly about the streets of Rome! IV, iv, 9–15

His last line is as practical and sensible as the remarks exchanged by Lear's daughters.[1] The final parallel to 'King Lear' is the rescue of the empire, but not of Titus and Lavinia who are both dead before the victory is assured, by an invading army led by the old man's youngest child.

[1] Cf. *Regan*: 'Tis the infirmity of his age:...
   Goneril: ... Then must we look to receive from his age ... the unruly wayward-
   ness that infirm and choleric years bring with them.
   Regan: Such unconstant starts are we like to have from him as this of Kent's
   banishment.   I, i, 296–305

It is interesting, but not now surprising, to find a whole phrase recurring to Shakespeare when he wrote the later play:

> I am not mad; I know thee well enough;[1]
>
> *Titus Andronicus*, v, i, 21

says Titus, during his terrible conversation with Tamora disguised as Revenge, and later he confesses:

> we wordly men
> Have miserable, mad, mistaking eyes.[2]   v, ii, 65–6

The eye-imagery which was later to determine the course of the sub-plot in *King Lear* has here appeared side by side with the theme of justice which is thus related to the truth or falsehood of appearances in Shakespeare's earliest tragedy.

Henry VI is also a significant forerunner of King Lear, for he is a king who signally fails to fulfil his obligations, and who divides his authority among those to whom it does not belong and who are incapable of exercising it properly. Lear demanded the pomp and circumstance and personal freedom which are the concomitants of royalty, but no man can 'retain the name, and all the additions to a king' by giving away the power, along with the responsibilities of kingship, and his elementary error is obvious to the audience as well as to the Fool:

> ... I can tell why a snail has a house. .... Why, to put his head in; not to give it away to his daughters, and leave his horns without a case.
>
> *King Lear*, I, v, 30–3

Henry's final error is—like Lear's first—the division of his kingdom between two 'younger strengths'. A refusal to exercise his proper power has been Henry's fault from the beginning of his reign, and the moment when Warwick and Clarence kneel before him, as Albany and Cornwall kneel before Lear, makes this statement in its most dramatically powerful form.

> Warwick and Clarence, give me both your hands:
> Now join your hands, and with your hands your hearts,

---

[1] Cf. 'I know thee well enough; thy name is Gloucester' (IV, vi, 181).

[2]   *Gloucester*: I have no way, and therefore want no eyes;
>   I stumbled when I saw.   IV, i, 20–1

> That no dissension hinder government:
> I make you both protectors of this land,
> While I myself will lead a private life
> And in devotion spend my latter days,
> To sin's rebuke and my Creator's praise.
>
> *3 Henry VI*, IV, vi, 38–44

Not only does he divide his kingdom into two instead of ruling it himself, but he bases his hopes of peace on misapprehensions very similar to Lear's.

> I have not stopp'd mine ears to their demands,
> Nor posted off their suits with slow delays;
> My pity hath been balm to heal their wounds,
> My mildness hath allay'd their swelling griefs,
> My mercy dried their water-flowing tears;...
> Then why should they love Edward more than me?
> No, Exeter, these graces challenge grace.   IV, viii, 39–48

After his final defeat Henry's words to the Lieutenant of the Tower who has begged his pardon are also paralleled in *King Lear*:

> For what, lieutenant? For well using me?
> Nay, be thou sure I'll well requite thy kindness,
> For that it made my imprisonment a pleasure;
> Ay, such a pleasure as incaged birds
> Conceive when after many moody thoughts
> At last by notes of household harmony
> They quite forget their loss of liberty.[1]   IV, vi, 9–15

Lastly, each of these royal victims is granted an extraordinary access of bodily vigour just before death; but while Henry uses this strength in the obvious way, to defy his enemy, Lear, although he kills the slave that was hanging Cordelia, yet uses his failing powers to carry in his arms the child he has himself sacrificed and, like an Abraham for whom there is no ram allowed in the thickets, to lay her on the ground and mourn for her, before he dies in the spiritual insight that her life and death have brought him.

We first see Lear, as we first see Othello, standing at the climax of his life. Both men, unable to distinguish good from evil, assume

---

[1] Cf. *King Lear*, V, ii, 8–19, and see below, p. 158.

the right to pass judgment and so provoke their own destruction by condemning the goodness they have failed to recognise. Lear's situation lacks the full irony of Othello's, however; he does not think he has penetrated to the inner truth of goodness beneath an appearance of evil nor of evil beneath the mask of goodness; he only makes the more common error of accepting appearances at their face value. He is also unlike Othello because, since the sentence he passes is one of banishment, not death, he is given time to discover the truth and make some measure of atonement.

The play opens with Lear in the role of a monarch whose 'robes and furr'd gown' hide the hollowness of his claim to true kingship. His sin is indeed so 'plated with gold' that 'the strong lance of justice', in the hands of Cordelia or Kent, 'hurtless breaks' against him.[1] He is himself represented by that great image of authority, the farmyard dog, which he later describes to Gloucester; he obeys his own whims and is swayed by his personal emotions, so that he both abuses the powers of his office and neglects its obligations. Finally, after the division of the kingdom he openly demands the shows of kingship when he has shuffled off its burdens. Lear has become as false a figure of authority as Angelo and knows himself as little.

In *King Lear* as in *Othello*, Authority, itself a mere simulacrum, fails to distinguish the genuine from the false in what it looks on, and Lear's Calvary starts quite simply because, from among the three women facing him, he fails to pick out the one who was good as well as beautiful, whose appearance was, in fact, her truth.

> *Lear*: So young, and so untender?
> *Cordelia*: So young, my lord, and true.
> *Lear*: Let it be so; thy truth, then, be thy dower.
>
> I, i, 108–10

To him her truth is the Nothing from which nothing can be made, and he goes on to commit the very same sin against the bonds of nature for which he later curses his other daughters.

> Here I disclaim all my paternal care,
> Propinquity and property of blood,

[1] *King Lear*, IV, vi, 169–70.

143

> And as a stranger to my heart and me
> Hold thee, from this, for ever.   I, i, 115–18

Cordelia is bound to resist Lear's demand because it is essentially an
impious one. He has sought for himself the absolute devotion
which is due only to God. The seeds of the later madness are already
in him, for his demand is that of a megalomaniac. Goneril and
Regan care nothing for what is involved. Regan can declare without a qualm that she is

> alone felicitate
> In your dear highness' love.   I, i, 77–8

At that moment, Lear, although he is still seated on the throne
which he thinks is his by right, is in reality a Lucifer figure, usurping
the position of the Almighty and completely unworthy of the
homage he receives from the evil spirits bowing before him.

> Better thou
> Hadst not been born than not to have pleased me better.
>   I, i, 236–7

cannot properly be said by one human being to another. Cordelia
offers the proportionate love, which is the right and beautiful thing
in a particular situation, and she offers it moreover *in perfection*:

> I love your majesty
> According to my bond; nor more nor less.   I, i, 94–5

It is for this that she is banished. It is no thanks to her father that
Cordelia does not leave the palace as desolate a wanderer as he was
soon to be. He says to her suitors:

> Will you, with those infirmities she owes,
> Unfriended, new-adopted to our hate,
> Dower'd with our curse, and stranger'd with our oath,
> Take her, or leave her?
>   ...for by the power that made me,
> I tell you all her wealth.   I, i, 205–11

Cordelia is saved only because France is at hand and recognises her
for what she is.

> Fairest Cordelia, that art most rich, being poor;

144

Most choice, forsaken; and most loved, despised!
Thee and thy virtues here I seize upon:
Be it lawful I take up what's cast away.   I, i, 253–6

Cordelia was indeed cast away by Lear, as truly as was Desdemona by the 'base Indian'.

One pattern—doubtless only one among several—which serves to show the unity within the multiplicity of *King Lear*, is made up of the threads under consideration here—justice, mercy and false-seeming. Lear's experience leads him to see ever more deeply beneath the skin of appearances, and at each level of knowledge he seeks vainly for justice until he comes to deny its existence. After his descent to these depths new knowledge is at last vouchsafed to him; it comes 'as a gift, as a grace', and after its advent he accepts for himself the new-discovered justice only to see it transcended by mercy in a world dominated by forgiveness and love.

The process of Lear's discovery of reality is slow. Beneath the semblances of false-seeming he discovers first the nature and reality of evil. The quarrel with Goneril begins with his comment on a change in her appearance; her beauty no longer dazzles him.

How now, daughter! what makes that frontlet on? Methinks you are too much of late i' the frown.   I, iv, 207–9

Her visage has already become in his eyes 'wolfish', and below the 'grace, health, beauty' of which she had boasted so glibly he sees her hidden reality.

Ingratitude, thou marble-hearted fiend,
More hideous when thou show'st thee in a child
Than the sea-monster!   I, iv, 281–3

He now understands that from her he cannot receive even the simple justice which would be a return in kind for his material gifts, still less generosity or affection. When Lear reaches Regan he shows that he understands the true quality of the love which he had once refused. He first asks of her what Cordelia had offered freely:

The offices of nature, bond of childhood.   II, iv, 181

Only after that does he appeal to a sense of obligation for benefits received, the 'dues of gratitude', and makes the half-trustful, half-fearful assertion:

> Thy half o' the kingdom hast thou not forgot,
> Wherein I thee endow'd.   II, iv, 183–4

All that he reads, however, in those eyes which he had believed so confidently would 'comfort and not burn', is the coldness of complete egoism. Regan accepts her half of the kingdom as no more than her due:

> Lear: I gave you all—
> Regan: And in good time you gave it.   II, iv, 253

Lear now becomes as acutely aware of Regan's appearance as he had earlier been of Goneril's and as concerned, though from a different point of view, with the contrast between appearance and reality:

> thou art a lady;
> If only to go warm were gorgeous,
> Why, nature needs not what thou gorgeous wear'st
> Which scarcely keeps thee warm.   II, iv, 270–3

The appearance is again different from what lies beneath it, but Lear's argument now runs that the appearance *should* be different. The flesh beneath the dress needs warmth only; to it the beauty of the dress is irrelevant, but the mind, which he distinguishes from the body although he knows it suffers with it, needs to be not only warm but 'gorgeous' too. On this plane appearances are truly relevant for they should represent the 'effects of courtesy' to which Lear had earlier appealed and which are essential to the life which, in distinction from that of the beasts, demands for its fulfilment more than the warmth of the sty and the food of the trough. When Lear, like the Prodigal Son, was reduced to these levels his case was pitiable indeed:

> ... and wast thou fain, poor father,
> To hovel thee with swine, and rogues forlorn,
> In short and musty straw?   IV, vii, 38–40

Regan's gorgeousness was not wrong in itself, any more than

146

was Goneril's beauty, but it was as treacherous because below her human clothing Regan was in fact no better than a beast. When Lear sees the naked Bedlam on the heath, he decides (wrongly as he later learns) that true man is 'unaccommodated man': that he is, as Edgar shows him to be, 'a poor, bare, forked animal', and that every restraint on his animality is merely 'sophistication', a gorgeous raiment which deceives only fools. In fact Lear is again deceived by false-seeming, this time a false-seeming in reverse, for under Edgar's degraded exterior lies hidden the true humanity which Lear needed so urgently to discover. But now in a desperate attempt to find the answer to his earlier question:

> Who is it that can tell me who I am? I, iv, 250

Lear starts to strip himself of all that hides his newly found illusion of truth:

> Off, off, you lendings! come, unbutton here. III, iv, 113–14

It is the fool who saves him from the futile ignominy:

> Prithee, nuncle, be contented; 'tis a naughty night to swim in.
> III, iv, 115–16

Whilst he can receive and, in a measure, return love, even the love of a fool, Lear does not act on his own dictum that man is a poor, bare, forked animal and nothing more. Here is the ray that points through the darkness to the moment when, in his heaviness, fresh garments will be put upon him and a new Lear will recognise Cordelia at last for what she is and be accepted by her. When Lear first realises that Goneril's beauty does not suffice to separate its owner from the beasts his new awareness of reality enables him to reassess the value of Cordelia's plain statement and his own response to it, so that he admits:

> I did her wrong. I, v, 25

He does not, however, understand the implications and extent of his error and still believes with spiritual complacency that he is 'more sinned against than sinning'. He can therefore continue to seek justice with confidence, and since it is denied him by man he commits his case to the gods:

> O heavens,
> If you do love old men...
> Make it your cause; send down, and take my part!
>
> II, iv, 192–5

Now he thinks he sees his own values disowned by heaven and his enemies' justified. The ministers of the gods, if not the gods themselves, have

> ...with two pernicious daughters join'd
> Your high engender'd battles 'gainst a head
> So old and white as this.   III, ii, 22–4

At the beginning of the storm he can cry:

> Tremble, thou wretch,
> That hast within thee undivulged crimes,
> Unwhipp'd of justice: hide thee, thou bloody hand;
> Thou perjured, and thou simular man of virtue
> That art incestuous: caitiff, to pieces shake,
> That under covert and convenient seeming
> Hast practised on man's life: close pent-up guilts,
> Rive your concealing continents, and cry
> These dreadful summoners grace.   III, ii, 51–9

But such counsel appears to be unnecessary; the simular men of virtue remain safe and undiscovered; it is the naked wretches and those whose clothes are only looped and windowed raggedness, together with a 'poor, infirm, weak and despised old man', who bear the pelting of the pitiless storm.

This storm has been heralded, however, by thoughts of *need* rather than by thoughts of justice. It is at the end of the speech containing the lines:

> But, for true need,—
> You heavens, give me that patience, patience I need!
>
> II, iv, 273–4

that the Folio places for the first time the stage direction: 'storm and tempest', and it is *the necessity* of the storm which must be recognised before its true relationship to justice and mercy can be apprehended. While Lear considers the storm as a final revelation of the 'horrible pleasure' of unjust gods, Kent considers it more simply as an intolerable burden:

> man's nature cannot carry
> The affliction nor the fear.   III, ii, 48–9

But both men are mistaken; the storm may indeed kill the fool, but it does not kill Lear; he endures it. The storm was in fact related to *Lear's need*. He was a man of unusual physical strength, as A. C. Bradley pointed out long ago; even at the age of eighty his powers were greater than those of many a man in his prime, and his passions were equally violent. His trial was in proportion to his strength, and his ordeal by lightning and by rain was a baptism of fire and water through which he passed alive. It would seem that nothing less violent than the storm could have redeemed Lear; it was his true need, for it was necessary for his salvation.

Sympathy with Lear is so intense when he is driven from Gloucester's door that it is tempting to accept the storm as the answer to his need and to probe no further, but the storm must also be viewed in relation to Lear's sin. This was not only against Cordelia; it was against humanity itself and hence was a symbol of sin against man's Creator, more potent even than that of rebellion against the king upon his throne. When Lear curses Goneril he is attempting to destroy the future generation.

> Hear, nature, hear; dear goddess, hear!
> Suspend thy purpose, if thou didst intend
> To make this creature fruitful!
> Into her womb convey sterility!
> Dry up in her the organs of increase;
> And from her derogate body never spring
> A babe to honour her!   I, iv, 297–303

Because she has struck him 'serpent-like upon the very heart', he calls on Heaven to 'strike her young bones...with lameness'; that is to say the bones of her unborn child. His first reaction in the agony of the storm is to repeat in universal terms this malediction.

> Crack nature's moulds, all germens spill at once,
> That make ingrateful man!   III, ii, 8–9

It is the same blasphemy against the essence of life that Macbeth makes in his final apostrophe to the witches:

> though the treasure
> Of nature's germens tumble all together,
> Even till destruction sicken; answer me
> To what I ask you.   IV, i, 58-61

Human imagination boggles at an attempt to conceive either a just punishment or an adequate means of purgation for this apostasy from the race of which the individual is a part. It is at least possible that Shakespeare in condemning Lear to suffer the storm and in allowing such a punishment to fit him for forgiveness after it, captured his ultimate vision of the horrific terms upon which the dichotomy of justice and mercy may be at last resolved.

It is at this point that Lear receives from Edgar the false revelation of the hidden reality of man's animal nature, on which he bases the terrifying indictment of the human race which he later makes to Gloucester. At the moment, however, the obsessional concern with his daughters reabsorbs his mind, and he passes on to enact the piteous travesty of human justice which takes place in Goucester's outhouse. He admits now an element of justice in his own plight but he does not yet recognise the true nature of his sin, for he believes it to be a sin of the flesh, the sexual act itself in which his children were conceived. He has no knowledge yet of his spiritual sins of pride and lack of love.

> Is it the fashion, that discarded fathers
> Should have thus little mercy on their flesh?
> Judicious punishment! 'twas this flesh begot
> Those pelican daughters.   III, iv, 74-7

It is still the condemnation of his daughters which he desires, this time from 'unaccommodated man', the fool, the madman and the servant, that humble triune commission of 'yoke-fellows in equity', exalted into the seats of the mighty. They were offering him freely what he really needed—forgiveness for their wrongs and pity for his own, but these were gifts which Lear could not yet receive; he was living in a cold, dark world, empty of all kindness.

> The little dogs and all,
> Tray, Blanch, and Sweet-heart, see, they bark at me.
>
> III, vi, 65–6

In spite of the fool's shrill singing, Edgar's mutterings and screechings and Kent's deep voice begging him to lie down and rest upon the cushions, Lear pursues his fruitless quest.

> I'll see their trial first.... Arraign her first; 'tis Goneril....
> And here's another, whose warp'd looks proclaim
> What store her heart is made on. III, vi, 37–57

But it is only to see his fantasy crumble before his eyes:

> Stop her there!
> Arms, arms, sword, fire! Corruption in the place!
> False justicer, why hast thou let her 'scape? III, vi, 57–9

Poor as his justicers are he is still curiously concerned with their clothes. They must not, after all, remain completely 'unaccommodated', for justice is unknown to the animals. One of them, covered in a blanket perhaps, becomes a 'robed man of justice', and another he criticises for his shabbiness.

> I do like not the fashion of your garments: you will say they are Persian attire; but let them be changed. III, vi, 84–6

It is after the failure of this trial of Goneril and Regan that Lear gives to Gloucester a final summing-up of his negative philosophy of man as an animal and of its relation to the concept of justice which it renders ultimately ridiculous: 'a dog's obeyed in office' (IV, vi, 163). When he says this Lear identifies himself with his opposites in the play. The pattern of an organised society which he here derides is exactly the one which Edmund both derides and ignores.

> Wherefore should I
> Stand in the plague of custom, and permit
> The curiosity of nations to deprive me,
> For that I am some twelve or fourteen moonshines
> Lag of a brother? Why bastard? wherefore base?
> When my dimensions are as well compact,

151

> My mind as generous, and my shape as true,
> As honest madam's issue?   I, ii, 2–9

Edmund is a particularly fine 'forked animal', as both Goneril and
Regan recognise, but as he deliberately refuses to be anything more
he becomes unsatisfactory to them even on that level:

> To both these sisters have I sworn my love;
> Each jealous of the other, as the stung
> Are of the adder. Which of them shall I take?
> Both? one? or neither?   v, i, 55–8

Edmund and his mistresses alike pride themselves on their ability to
recognise facts, unblinded even by their own hatred and envy:

> *Edmund*: A credulous father! and a brother noble,
>   ...I see the business.   I, ii, 195–8

Goneril: ...he always loved our sister most; and with what poor judge-
ment he hath now cast her off appears too grossly.   I, i, 293–5

Like Gertrude, they are all three convinced that 'all that is' they see,
yet it is the hidden truth their shrewdness misses which at last destroys them. Goneril and Regan die because their assessment of a
situation they think they well understand fails to allow for the
driving-force of their own lusts, and Edmund because the brother
whom he thought he could manipulate like a puppet, returns at
last to challenge and defeat him.

It is Lear himself, however, who realises and describes more
clearly even than his enemies the full consequences of accepting
true man as animal man. In madness his knowledge of his body is
the only certainty that remains to him.

When the rain came to wet me once, and the wind to make me chatter;
when the thunder would not peace at my bidding; there I found 'em,
there I smelt 'em out....they told me I was every thing; 'tis a lie, I am
not ague-proof.   IV, vi, 102–7

Again he thinks of clothes as a pretence at dignity, a vain disguise
of reality.

> Behold yond simpering dame,
> Whose face between her forks[1] presages snow;

[1] Head-dress.

152

... The fitchew, nor the soiled horse, goes to't
With a more riotous appetite.
But to the girdle do the gods inherit,
Beneath is all the fiends.   IV, vi, 120–8

To such beings sin is an impossibility.

Thou shalt not die: die for adultery! No:
The wren goes to't, and the small gilded fly
Does lecher in my sight.
Let copulation thrive.   IV, vi, 113–16

Our common animality, common also to the beast, makes us all
alike.

Thou rascal beadle, hold thy bloody hand!
Why does thou lash that whore? Strip thine own back;
Thou hotly lust'st to use her in that kind
For which thou whipp'st her. The usurer hangs the cozener.
Through tatter'd clothes small vices do appear;
Robes and furr'd gowns hide all.   IV, vi, 164–9

Therefore justice becomes both unnecessary and impossible, a
chimera with which to frighten children—no more.

None does offend, none, I say, none. I'll able 'em.   IV, vi, 172

For a moment Lear's outlook seems to be identified with that of the
Duke of Vienna who does 'able' even Angelo at the end of *Measure
for Measure*. But the duke had judged the sinner and waited for
penitence before he offered mercy. Lear is denying the need for
either justice or mercy, because he is denying all moral values; he is
pointing to the wilderness in which those who think of a bond as a
thing to escape from, of 'custom' and 'the effects of courtesie, dues
of gratitude' as nuisances to be avoided in the search for success, will
surely find themselves. It is for the hand of this Lear that Gloucester
feels in order that he may kiss it, and the poignant ambiguity of
Lear's picture of humanity is clear in his response. He accepts the
kiss—that symbol of all gracious ceremony and of reaches of both
love and treachery equally unknown to the beasts—but he does not
forget his animal flesh as he does so:

Let me wipe it first; it smells of mortality.   IV, vi, 136

153

L

When Lear awakes from his madness and reaches at last as much knowledge of the reality behind bodily seeming as humanity can endure, he believes at first that he is bound upon a wheel of fire suffering the punishment of eternal damnation and that Cordelia is a visiting spirit from Paradise. He makes no appeal against the justice of this, but when he seeks Cordelia's forgiveness and accepts her love the two of them move together into a world where justice is transcended in pity and forgiveness.

> Had you not been their father, these white flakes
> Had challenged pity of them. Was this a face
> To be opposed against the warring winds?
>   ... Mine enemy's dog,
> Though he had bit me, should have stood that night
> Against my fire.   IV, vii, 30–8

It is characteristic of the last part of this play that Shakespeare should often rely on theatrical symbols rather than on the spoken word. The great challenge of right to wrong, presented with all the panoply of the medieval duel between Edgar and Edmund, is of course the principal instance, for here Childe Roland visibly as well as audibly winds his horn before the Dark Tower, and Lucifer is challenged by Michael to doubtful battle on the plains of Britain. It is as though after the poetry of the storm scenes other weapons were necessary for the next assault on an audience's responses. It is in line with this technique that in his meeting with Cordelia Lear finds hardly more words with which to seek her forgiveness than she does with which to answer him:

> *Lear*: I know you do not love me; for your sisters
> Have, as I do remember, done me wrong:
> You have some cause, they have not.
> *Cordelia*: No cause, no cause.   IV, vii, 73–6

But the significance of the scene depends on Lear's kneeling to the daughter whom he had once repudiated, and that action must be fully exploited so that it may bear all the weight that Shakespeare intended it to carry. It is not right for the actor to do no more than stumble forward out of his chair, and be immediately restored to it by the attendants. The king must kneel right down as Cordelia has already done; they should both still be kneeling when he touches her eyes and finds them wet and when he says:

If you have poison for me, I will drink it.   IV, vii, 172

Kent should raise him on the line: 'In your own kingdom, sir', so that the king is in Kent's arms when he begs: 'Do not abuse me', a picture beautifully in keeping with Kent's role, which needs any strengthening that can be afforded it by visual means in this part of the play. A small but not unimportant point is that if Lear is standing, leaning on Kent, during the doctor's speech, Cordelia's line: 'Will't please your highness walk?' becomes a natural invitation, instead of the ungracious forcing of the old man to his feet which it too often appears to be on the stage. It is peculiarly poignant if her words are prompted as they should be, by Lear's stumbling attempt to reach her arms—the first hesitating steps of the old man become a child again. Shakespeare never bungles an exit, and even if the symbolism did not demand it, this line alone would indicate that the king kneels so long that it is unnecessary for him to sit again before the end of the scene. Lear has already knelt once before—in the horrible parody of humility before Regan by which he achieves a self-mockery hardly endurable to witness; even Cornwall finds it unpleasant. Only Kent, besides the king, is present in both scenes, and in a play so full of echoes and reflections it is likely that Shakespeare intended Kent to raise his master on both occasions, using the same reverent and protective movement—one which the king must ignore the first time but accept with humble gratitude on the second.

When Lear offers to drink poison at Cordelia's hands, he is not seeking to escape from the realities of life and 'unburthen'd crawl toward death' as he attempted to do at the beginning of the play. The memory of *Measure for Measure* enforces a positive not a negative interpretation of Lear's words. As we have seen, the duke of Vienna set himself the task of persuading Claudio, Angelo and Barnardine to accept death willingly because such an acceptance was the prerequisite for a new life. In the earlier play the thought is naturalistically presented in terms of self-knowledge, repentance and the desire to make atonement which properly follows the admission of guilt. The treatment in *King Lear* stands between this convention and the more formal symbolism of the last plays. We watch Lear on the heath and in his madness enduring the symbolic death which is pictured as the passage to maturity in every baptism, whether Christian or pagan, and which must be accepted as a necessary step to full life.

> Therefore we are buried with him by baptism into death: that...so we also should walk in newness of life.[1]

In the light of this imagery it should be clear that when Lear could have said as Angelo did:

> I crave death more willingly than mercy,
> *Measure for Measure*, v, i, 481[2]

his desire for this death should be viewed not as an attempt to retreat from reality but as a step towards its discovery.

Edgar and Edmund make the final magnificent statement of the inevitability of justice in a duet for two voices ending with a perfect cadence.

> *Edgar*:   Let's exchange charity....
> My name is Edgar, and thy father's son.
> The gods are just, and of our pleasant vices
> Make instruments to plague us:
> The dark and vicious place where thee he got
> Cost him his eyes.
> *Edmund*:   Thou hast spoken right, 'tis true;
> The wheel is come full circle; I am here.   v, iii, 166–74

The opening dialogue of the play is suddenly illuminated. We realise the full irony of Kent's well-meaning but imperceptive: 'I cannot wish the fault undone, the issue of it being so proper' and Gloucester's complacent, 'the whoreson must be acknowledged' (I, i, 17–24). The apparent ruthlessness of Edgar's words is in line with Cordelia's when she offers love according to her bond. It must

---

[1] Romans, vi, 4.   [2] See above, p. 115.

always be allowed its full imaginative weight in apprehending the play's pattern. Only after evil has been seen for what it is can goodness also be fully known; only when sin is acknowledged can it be forgiven.

We never hear Edmund ask for mercy, but we do see him render a 'deed of mercy'. He renders it, so it appears, reluctantly, and he renders it late—almost with his last breath: 'I pant for life.' Rendering mercy and seeking it, however, have been before so closely linked in the pleadings of Portia and of Isabella that perhaps Shakespeare's imagination made the association also in his conception of Edmund. Moreover, Edmund has been offered forgiveness by Edgar, and though there is no direct evidence that he accepts it, there is none that he refuses; one or the other he is almost bound to do, by implication, on the stage. His deed of mercy comes too late to save Lear and Cordelia, but does it come too late to save himself? Admittedly Shakespeare does not show us clearly, but perhaps his intentions can be inferred. There was no need for a *volte-face* from Edmund in order that word of Cordelia's peril should be brought from the prison; the fact that Shakespeare finds space for it suggests that he felt it to be important. How can it be so if not as evidence that Edmund submits himself to the divine pattern and recognising his own need of mercy attempts to render it at last? His movement towards good is clumsy and ineffective; he has no time to grow in grace, but unless Shakespeare meant our imaginations to take a final leap with his and accept the reality of Edmund's salvation, why—in this desperately crowded moment of his play— did he spend time in leading us so far along that path? If this interpretation is correct it is not without interest, for Edmund would be the only exemplar of Lucifer to find forgiveness before Antonio in *The Tempest*, and this example of salvation would strengthen the link between *King Lear* and the romances and therefore support the belief that the latter are statements of Shakespeare's imaginative vision as genuine as those of the tragedies.

When Lear enters the new world in which he finds Cordelia again, he quite forgets his old passionate desire for justice. Cordelia would choose to face their enemies: 'Shall we not see these daughters and these sisters?' But Lear values nothing now except his new and precious joy.

> No, no, no, no! Come, let's away to prison:
> We two alone will sing like birds i' the cage:
>   ...Have I caught thee?
> He that parts us shall bring a brand from heaven,
> And fire us hence like foxes.   v, iii, 8–23

In this scene it is peculiarly hard to be sure of Shakespeare's intention. Two incompatible interpretations appear to be possible. One is that we have here another of Lear's divagations from the direct path towards truth. Certainly he appears to make again the same demand for total devotion which Cordelia rightly refused at the beginning of the play, and this time apparently she grants it, in spite of the fact that she is now married and had insisted that her husband would have a right to half her love and duty. It may be argued that it is right for her to grant to his weakness what she denied to his strength, yet the demand that she live with him like a captive bird in a cage, singing so sweetly only because its eyes have been put out, may well be condemned as wrong and even horrible. And this is not merely a subjective judgment; it stems from the play's own implications concerning the father–child relationship in its first act. Lear's progress from his initial fault to his final redemption has been marked, as we have seen, by repeated excursions into error and half-truth, so that there is nothing in the play's structure to prevent such a movement here. Nevertheless, the present writer remains deeply uncertain of its propriety. It will be remembered that Henry VI compared his pleasure in prison to that enjoyed by caged birds who by their 'household harmony ... forget their loss of liberty'.[1] Harmony is always suggestive of goodness to Shakespeare, so it is possible that to him the song in prison images the joy found in total submission to the whole 'in whose service' only 'is perfect freedom'. Intense sympathy for Lear seems the spontaneous attitude of everyone directly involved in the acting of the scene, and on the stage sympathy and direct condemnation are rare and

[1] See above, p. 142.

uneasy companions. The conclusive evidence remains that of the plot. For Lear and Cordelia there was no alternative to prison at this point. Lear's demand was therefore that necessity should be accepted with readiness and he had come to believe that such acceptance brought the harmony of joy and peace. Moreover, in that necessity all his earlier 'goods' except the one 'good' of his daughter's love have disappeared. The measure of the length of his journey is that he no longer even remembers their loss. He is granted a moment of bliss in which necessity and desire coincide.

An even more important crux of interpretation is concerned with the alternative endings to the play in the Quarto and Folio texts. The difference between these two versions of the death of Lear is not merely a textual enigma; it profoundly affects the conclusion of the play. In the first Quarto the lines run thus:

Lear: . . . no, no life, why should a dog, a horse, a rat of life and thou no
breath at all, O thou wilt come no more, never, never, never, pray you
undo this button, thanke you sir, O, o, o, o,
Edgar: He faints, my lord, my lord.
Lear: Breake heart, I prethe breake.

This is the moment of Lear's death and its significance is that he dies, no longer hoodwinked by his own clouded vision or reality's multiple disguises. This is his triumph: Cordelia teaches him in death, as she had failed to do in life, the truth both of the reality of love and of its brevity, and in face of this, the crucial paradox of human life, he desires and is granted death.

In the Folio we read as follows:

> *Lear:*　no no no life?
> Why should a Dog, a Horse, a Rat have life,
> And thou no breath at all? Thou'lt come no more,
> Never, never, never, never, never.
> Pray you undo this button. Thank you Sir,
> Do you see this? Look on her? Look her lips
> Look there, look there.
> ### He dies
> *Edgar:* He faints, my Lord, my Lord.
> *Kent:* Break heart, I prithee break.

Here the final impression is different. Whatever the significance of Lear's absorption in his newly recovered treasure may be, such quintessential bliss cannot endure on earth, yet here Lear dies in joy because of the faith that his treasure by its very nature transcends mortality. In this world, or in another, he believes Cordelia lives. On the words 'Look there, look there', his eyes are not necessarily on her face. Perhaps it is outside her body that he sees her waiting for him—the Form itself of love, which can never be destroyed though every individual Cordelia must perish.

If the Quarto, printed in 1606, represents Shakespeare's first version, it is possible that a concern with immortality, traceable in the last plays, led him back to *King Lear* to add another colour to its already fantastically complex palette. If so, he revived an element of the story of *Measure for Measure* and gave us one more image of the man who, after he has accepted the necessity of death, discovers life at last.[1]

The likeness of *Timon of Athens* to *King Lear* in characterisation and imagery is fully accepted; here we need only realise that it uses half the *King Lear* material, not all of it. The central situation of *Timon of Athens* shows a search in which the seeker, goaded to the last miseries of desperation by his wrongs, is yet never rewarded by finding either justice or mercy. Timon is not even saved the full contemplation of this horror by madness. He may well think with Gloucester: 'Better I were distract', but he is spared no knowledge of the evil which surrounds him. In spite of this, however, he never slips into the amorality which for a time clouds Lear's vision. Evil is always as evil to him as it is ubiquitous. He makes the demand of *Measure for Measure* for the upright judge:

Who dares, who dares,

---

[1] The many parallels between *King Lear* and *Cymbeline* make a comparison of interest here. When Cymbeline realises that the fainting page-boy is really his daughter and that she is alive he cries:

If this be so, the gods do mean to strike me
To death with mortal joy.   v, v, 234–5

In this case the old father is not deceived and the fact perhaps reinforces the interpretation that Lear dies of joy believing Cordelia still breathes. The earlier naturalistic ending has also a close parallel, i.e. the short scene in which Talbot dies with the body of his son in his arms (*1 Henry VI*, IV, vii, 29–32).

> In purity of manhood stand upright,
> And say 'This man's a flatterer'? if one be,
> So are they all.
>
> *Timon of Athens*, IV, iii, 13–16

He sends the robbers to Athens with the words:

> The laws, your curb and whip, in their rough power
> Have uncheck'd theft....
> All that you meet are thieves: to Athens go,
> Break open shops; nothing can you steal,
> But thieves do lose it. IV, iii, 446–51

When Alcibiades calls out:

> What art thou there? speak. IV, iii, 48

Timon answers:

> A beast, as thou art. IV, iii, 49

But he never cries out like Lear, 'none does offend', only that none is fit to judge, and perhaps it is because he retains the knowledge that a man may sin that he is able to recognise also the goodness of the one man in the play who inhabits the same world as Cordelia. Even while Timon called down curses upon all inside the walls of Athens his servants were weeping for him, and Flavius set out to follow him. But although Timon unlike Lear could recognise his follower's goodness, it brought him no comfort.

> Had I a steward
> So true, so just, and now so comfortable?
> It almost turns my dangerous nature mild.
> Let me behold thy face. Surely, this man
> Was born of woman.
> Forgive my general and exceptless rashness,
> You perpetual-sober gods! I do proclaim
> One honest man—mistake me not—but one;
> No more, I pray,—and he's a steward.
> How fain would I have hated all mankind!
> And thou redeem'st thyself: ...
> Thou singly honest man,
> Here, take: the gods out of my misery

> Have sent thee treasure. Go, live rich and happy;
> But thus condition'd: thou shalt build from men;
> Hate all, curse all, show charity to none,
> But let the famish'd flesh slide from the bone,
> Ere thou relieve the beggar;...
>
>   be men like blasted woods,
> And may diseases lick up their false bloods!   IV, iii, 497–539

On the heath Lear was saved from stripping himself naked by accepting the love of the Fool; after his refusal of Flavius there is nothing left for Timon but death. His terrible passion of negation, with its determination to finish his 'long sickness of health and living' is the inevitable end of the strong man who seeks justice and refuses mercy for both himself and others.

> Come not to me again; but say to Athens,
> Timon has made his everlasting mansion
> Upon the beached verge of the salt flood;
> Who once a day with his embossed froth
> The turbulent surge shall cover:
>
>   ... Timon hath done his reign.   v, i, 217–26

Whenever *Timon of Athens* was actually written it appears unlikely that it was imaginatively conceived after *King Lear*. Without *The Tempest*, we might have been driven to believe that Shakespeare's imagination led him finally into Timon's world, a place whose ultimate reality was horror and where the 'unpublish'd virtues of the earth', though watered with the tears of goodness, never sprang to 'be aidant and remediate in the good man's distress'; where Kent and Cordelia, and even the Fool and Edgar, were only romantic illusions. But Lear does not die as Timon dies; he dies healed, and *The Tempest* remains to affirm that to the end of his working life Shakespeare retained the faith implicit in his greatest play, that in the ruling of 'the clearest gods', justice and mercy meet.

PART III

'A LASTING SPRING'

CHAPTER VI

THE TRANSITION

1. THE COMING OF BIRNAM WOOD

Macbeth; *Richard III*; *Titus Andronicus*; *King Lear*; *Hamlet*;
Antony and Cleopatra; *2 Henry IV*; *Henry VIII*; *Othello*

In *Macbeth* Shakespeare presents evil in a form more violent and apparently more impervious to challenge than that used by him in any other play, and against this evil he allows the forces of good to achieve their most signal victory. When Birnam Wood covers the bleak hills of Dunsinane the very earth itself 'blows into life's flower again', and men's ancient faith in the recurrent miracle of Spring is given *direct* presentation in English literary drama for the first time. Every year Shakespeare and the men and women of his audience would see young men and girls

Spring sooner than the lark to fetch in May.[1]

Every year they would see the 'Green Men', the 'Jacks in the Green', joining with the other dancers round the Maypole in celebrations which had lingered on from an immemorial worship of nature's fertility. In bringing the boughs of Birnam Wood against Macbeth's apparently impregnable fortress Shakespeare created the greatest theatrical image of the victory of life over death, and therefore of mercy over justice, that we can hope to see. This is the form in which he shows how 'The powers above put on their instruments'. The men who bear before them the boughs of Birnam Wood bring to the most death-ridden of the tragedies the most brilliant promise of life.

This pagan symbol of indestructible fertility is combined with Shakespeare's strongest dramatisation of the Christian Doomsday theme, and *Macbeth* is thus both the culminating play of a series

---

[1] Robert Herrick, *Corinna's Going a-Maying*.

which presents, in fundamentally Christian terms, the conflict between justice and mercy to determine mankind's fate and also the starting-point of a second series in which the imaginative quest for a solution of the human dilemma is sought along different paths.

Macbeth makes Shakespeare's most startling statement of that fundamental conflict between the forces of death and life which had first influenced his creative work in *The Comedy of Errors*. The light of mercy and hope is visibly triumphant in its final scenes, while the darkness imaged in those which precede them is deeper than that in any other of the plays. Here Shakespeare is not content with the traditional dogma that the wages of sin is death; he appears actually to identify evil not only with death for the individual but also with that of the race—the unborn children of the future. As Macbeth wades on in blood, killing becomes the only activity he can compass; it is his one reply to every threat. He becomes Death, the figure who struck with his dart at Herod[1] and at Everyman,[2] until he himself dies at last. Another statement of the same truth is made through the psychological development of the two protagonists. After they have killed Duncan a sentence of death is gradually carried out on Macbeth and Lady Macbeth while they live. Their vital energy decreases, and this is revealed most clearly in their relationship with each other. Duncan has noticed its quality when the play opens, for he says of her husband to Lady Macbeth:

> ... his great love, sharp as his spur, hath holp him
> To his home before us.   I, vi, 23–4

Macbeth writes the whole story of his encounter with the witches to his 'dearest partner of greatness', but he changes after that night

> Which shall to all our nights and days to come
> Give solely sovereign sway and masterdom.   I, v, 70–1

He turns to her once with the words 'dear wife', and she is still his 'dearest chuck' when he is deceiving her about Banquo's presence at the feast, but this is all, and she becomes at last simply a woman who 'should have died hereafter', whose death provokes in him no more than images of life's futility. She herself declines from the

---

[1] *Ludus Coventriae, Death of Herod.*   [2] *Summoning of Everyman.*

passionate, vital creature who should 'bring forth men-children only', to the languid, exhausted woman whose pallid sentences after the haunted banquet are hardly noticed by her husband, and finally to the muttering guilt-ridden sleep-walker and the despairing suicide.

The same association between evil and the loss of vitality is emphasised in the play by all that concerns witchcraft and demonology; the invocation of evil spirits is an invocation of death, not only in the present but in the future, for it is an invocation of sterility.

> Come, you spirits
> That tend on mortal thoughts, unsex me here.   I, V, 41–2

The question, 'How many children had Lady Macbeth?' is not so foolish as it has been made to sound. It is of great significance that Lady Macbeth had borne a child and that in order to achieve her purposes she was willing to give up the power of bearing another. She associates her husband's humanity with 'the milk of human kindness' and goes on deliberately to sacrifice her own future motherhood by the prayer:

> Come to my woman's breasts,
> And take my milk for gall.   I, V, 48–9

James I declared that a witch's charms might 'stay married folk to have natural ado with each other'[1] and Reginald Scott reported that witches could 'take away men's courage and power of generation'.[2] There are many signs that Shakespeare had read both books, and it is significant that it is not Macbeth but Banquo who plants the seed of the future. Lady Macbeth is well aware that she is turning from life and health to disease. She believes that Macbeth is still 'without the illness' which should attend his ambition, but also that she can infect him with it as soon as she can pour her 'spirits in his ear'. Possibly a picture of Claudius bending over his sleeping brother was before Shakespeare's eyes as he wrote the words.

Both Macbeth and Lady Macbeth are aware of the context within which man's life can properly be lived. Unlike Goneril and

---

[1] *Demonology* (1597).   [2] *Discovery of Witchcraft* (1584).

Regan they would have understood Cordelia when she spoke of love according to her bond. Macbeth uses her very word. He knows he can only achieve the murder of Banquo if night with her 'bloody and invisible hand' will

> Cancel and tear to pieces that great bond
> Which keeps me pale!   III, ii, 49–50

The great bond is the natural law to which man, by virtue of his humanity, is subject and submission to which would have saved Macbeth. Lady Macbeth is also like Cordelia in so far as she recognises the bond particularly as it applies to personal relationships. She knows what it is to love father and child, and she is not able to forget it in the one case, although she claims that she could do so in the other:

> Had he not resembled
> My father as he slept, I had done't.   II, ii, 13–14

The lines about the baby at her breast have been used in the attempt to prove her depravity, but they prove the reverse. The most terrible act she could conceive of was the destruction of the child she had borne, and her words are an image of what she did in fact attempt to do. To the last, however, she preserves a trace of the forces of life which had once been so potent: in her sleep-walking she reveals that she still loves the husband for whom she had dared so much, and it must have been in part because he never answered her repeated: 'Come, come, come, come', that she finally 'fordid herself'. For Macbeth only a memory of the goodness he forswore remains and that but dimly. He recalls 'honour, love, obedience, troops of friends' (v, iii, 25), but they are a wish not an actuality. His hangman's hands had indeed plucked out his eyes as surely as they had murdered the sleep that brings men rest and healing.

Finally, the language—both that of direct statement and that of imagery—presents the murderers shrouded in the darkness of death and stained with the blood they continued to shed until theirs was shed in turn: 'sealing night', 'the blanket of the dark', 'scarf up the tender eye of pitiful day', 'pall thee in the dunnest smoke of hell', 'light thickens', 'hell is murky', 'on thy blade and dudgeon gouts of blood', 'their daggers unmannerly breeched with gore', 'his brandished steel which smoked with bloody execution', 'except they meant to bathe in reeking wounds'—the phrases pour into the mind. Macbeth is himself that bird of night, the mousing owl, who kills 'a falcon towering in her pride of place'. On the day following Duncan's death Ross asks:

> Is't night's predominance, or the day's shame,
> That darkness does the face of earth entomb,
> When living light should kiss it?   II, iv, 8–10

and in the centre of the play, just before the tide begins to flow, the night is

> almost at odds with morning, which is which.   III, iv, 127

It is in the imagery also that there is first conveyed the complementary truth. Blood is an ambiguous symbol, for a child may be born in blood as well as killed in it. Macduff, who brings life to Scotland, 'was from his mother's womb untimely ripp'd', and by the witches' magic he is shown as a babe covered with the blood of his mother's suffering.[1] This apparition is followed by that of a child 'crowned and with a tree in his hand' which leads to Macbeth's question concerning Banquo's issue. It is because he feared that his rival would be the *root* of many kings that Macbeth, brooding on his own *fruitless* crown and *barren* sceptre, had decided to murder him. But life is resistant to evil:

> Most royal sir,
> Fleance is 'scaped.   III, iv, 19–20

The child, wearing

> upon his baby-brow the round
> And top of sovereignty   IV, i, 88–9

is stronger than the 'armed Head' which harped Macbeth's fear aright,

> And pity, like a naked new-born babe

does in truth stride the blast, and

---

[1] It is particularly ironic that this apparition, which should have warned Macbeth of the truth, leads him to declare: 'Then live, Macduff; what need I fear of thee?' (v, i, 82).

horsed
Upon the sightless couriers of the air,
Shall blow the horrid deed in every eye,
That tears shall drown the wind.   I, vii, 21-6

Its frequent references to the might of the apparently helpless child make *Macbeth*—strange as it may at first sight appear—Shakespeare's Christmas play. 'Fleance is 'scaped' is a reminder of the well-known stage direction in the Coventry Nativity Pageant: 'Mary and Joseph goeth clean away.' Fleance doubles Malcolm's role in this respect, for Malcolm also 'goeth clean away', while little Macduff, like the Innocents of Bethlehem, dies in the place of the true prince, at the hands of unreasoning *hubris*.

The play does not content itself, however, with the hopes of Christmas and the Flight into Egypt; it shows the return of the royal exile. Malcolm comes back from a country which Shakespeare is at pains to associate with what has been well called 'the good super-natural'. Its king is the aged and saintly Edward the Confessor, and he it is who dispatches Duncan's son to deal out the dooms of reward and punishment and to reign at last in the kingdom from which he had been ejected and where Barabbas had been chosen in his stead. With Malcolm's return the life of nature rallies against its destroyer as inevitably as sap rises in the trees.

Within this three mile may you see it coming;
I say, a moving grove.   v, v, 37-8

The unique impression made by the ending of Macbeth depends in part on this combination of the images of natural fertility with those of Christian virtue, and Shakespeare appears to have seen no anomaly in such a union.

Malcolm's command rings out:

...your leavy screens throw down,
And show like those you are.   v, vi, 1-2

And what are they like, the men who challenge enthroned evil and conquer it? Fallible of course as all mortal instruments of 'the powers above' must be, but Shakespeare has described through

Malcolm the Christian virtues which they would wish to find within themselves:

> The king-becoming graces,
> As justice, verity, temperance, stableness,
> Bounty, perseverance, mercy, lowliness,
> Devotion, patience, courage, fortitude.   IV, iii, 91–4

The figure of Malcolm marks the highest point on a long curve; it is led up to by various exiled successors to a crown, and Shakespeare's development and subsequent modification of the medieval archetype of the Saviour Prince links his earliest plays with his last.

In *Richard III*, Henry Richmond—seen in *2 Henry VI* as the child who escapes to be preserved overseas—returns and wins his kingdom by his own right arm on Bosworth Field, killing the usurper in single combat. In *Titus Andronicus*, Lucius returns over the mountains, leading an army of rescue from abroad just as Henry did, but it is Titus who slays the wicked emperor and afterwards takes his own life, so that the task of Lucius is simply to establish peace: his own hands are clean of bloodshed, and it is his figure which is the prototype of the later 'Saviours'. Malcolm wins his own victory at Dunsinane, but the actual slaying of Macbeth is carried out by Macduff so that the prince who mounts the throne compassed by his 'kingdom's pearl' appears as innocent of bloodshedding. Edgar does not emerge from disguise in time to fight in the battle which brings him, with Albany, to the throne; he challenges Edmund and kills him by an 'honourable' form of violence, single combat. An awareness of the pattern presented so clearly in the other plays shows that although *King Lear* is primarily concerned with Lear's personal fall and redemption yet, viewed from another angle, the play also shows in social terms the necessary driving out of decay by new life. The splitting of this function of youth between the two brothers allows Edmund to destroy the 'old year' by violence and Edgar to avenge and succeed the king without the stain of compassing his death. *Hamlet*, in this as in other respects, offers an enigma. Its hero is himself a rejected prince who returns from across the water and succeeds in destroying the usurper, but the succession passes to Fortinbras, who arrives with an army of rescue which he does not need to use and whose hands, as far as Denmark is concerned, are clean of blood. Nevertheless, it is surely Hamlet who should inaugurate the new era and bring reward as well as punishment to his people, and possibly we have here a valuable clue to the origin of the play's many problems. In essentials the old legend, in spite of the depth of its psychological significance, did not offer Shakespeare the metaphysical pattern that he needed at the time he wrote this play. We miss in it the internal coherence of the story of Lear's redemption or Macbeth's damnation. However deep Shakespeare's psychological insight, the form of his plays appears to be determined less by individual characterisation than by typological significance. In conception Hamlet repeats the familiar figure of the young saviour, but the play's plot does not allow him to fulfil this role. Although the returning prince has a clearly Christian origin, yet the culture hero who departs and returns over the water finds his way into English literature from Teutonic and Celtic lands, not from the Middle East. Arthur and Beowulf are therefore prototypes here as well as the Hebrew Messiah, so that there is no revolutionary turn from Christian to pagan imagery when, in the romances, Shakespeare chooses not the exiled hero but the spring goddess as the symbol of renewed life.

After the apotheosis of the saviour prince in *Macbeth*, the figure changes, and Octavius and Alcibiades present it not only weakened but degraded; Octavius with his stratagems and smooth self-seeking is clearly opening an era of pygmies after one of giants, and in *Antony and Cleopatra* the passing of the old year cannot be rejoiced at but only mourned for.

> For his bounty,
> There was no winter in't; an autumn 'twas
> That grew the more by reaping.   v, ii, 86–8

Even lower sinks Alcibiades who leads the forces of righteous vengeance against Athens carrying with him his two whores, and who is bought off by the corrupt senators' first offers. The Shakespearean figures closest in function to their divine original are Henry Tudor, Lucius Andronicus and Malcolm, who all return after long exile to defeat an Antichrist, to reward, to punish and to reign. Fortinbras and Octavius stand on the fringe of the group, and behind them, equivocal as always, may be discerned the enigmatic, smiling face of Henry V. He was no alien and no rejected exile, but he came to his coronation from sojourning in a strange land, the stews of Eastcheap, and his return in 'this new and gorgeous garment, majesty' was radiant and full of promise:

> And, God consigning to my good intents,
> No prince nor peer shall have just cause to say,
> God shorten Harry's happy life one day!
>
> 2 Henry IV, v, ii, 143-5

Nevertheless, he brought his subjects no peaceful millennium but a violent and bloody war; in whatever setting he is considered he retains the essential ambiguity allotted him by his creator.

But Henry V is not Shakespeare's last picture of an English saviour. At the end of his life he wrote of the advent of the queen to whom her subjects had paid semi-divine honours even while she lived. Princess Elizabeth did not come to her people from over the sea, but she had been rejected and came, as they well knew, from very real perils. It is of interest that this last of Shakespeare's historical saviours is feminine. Cranmer's prophecy brings the baby princess into closer contact with Miranda than with Malcolm. Much of its haunting beauty is due to the paradoxical tributes to both chastity and fertility which appear also in the Romances. Attention is, however, focused on the millennium she will bring to her kingdom and her subjects, so that in spite of the overtones of seasonal ritual it is proper to place Shakespeare's Elizabeth among the political saviours.

> This royal infant—heaven still move about her!—
> Though in her cradle, yet now promises
> Upon this land a thousand thousand blessings,
> Which time shall bring to ripeness: she shall be—
> But few now living can behold that goodness—
> A pattern to all princes living with her,
> And all that shall succeed:...
> She shall be loved and fear'd...

> good grows with her:
> In her days every man shall eat in safety,
> Under his own vine, what he plants; and sing
> The merry songs of peace to all his neighbours:...
> She shall be, to the happiness of England,
> An aged princess; many days shall see her,
> And yet no day without a deed to crown it.
> Would I had known no more! but she must die,
> She must, the saints must have her; yet a virgin,
> A most unspotted lily shall she pass,
> To the ground, and all the world shall mourn her.
>
> *Henry VIII*, v, v, 18–63

An interesting link between the returning heroes of the Histories and the Tragedies and those of the Romances is found at the end of *Othello*. Lodovico arrives in the typical manner from over the sea to inaugurate the new era in Cyprus; it is not he but Cassio, however, who becomes the governor. Cassio has done nothing against his 'dear general'; on the contrary he stands to him in the relationship of a loved son. As the nature of the sin committed has, as it were, been contracted from the social to the personal world, so the bringer of renewed life moves from the world of politics into that of the closest personal relationships.[1] The romances, without exception, find a man's saviour in his own child, though the gift of renewed life to the father—who is also a king—spreads beyond him to his people.

2. A LASS UNPARALLEL'D

Antony and Cleopatra

After *Macbeth* the symbol of the usurped throne with all its religious and political associations ceases to be central in the plays. It has already been noted that Shakespeare never minimised the importance of the 'deeds of mercy' which man could render to man, and in his last plays the theological implications inherent in

---

[1] Certainly Lucius Andronicus is the son of Titus, but the fact is immaterial; any Roman exile could have taken his place.

the conception of kingship are undermined by the new emphasis placed on man's dependence, for good or ill, on his closest human associates. This development is foreshadowed in *Othello*, but it is first of major importance in *Antony and Cleopatra*. In this play Shakespeare not only places a man's public and private lives in explicit conflict but finally uses the events of his private, not his public, life to express the play's essential values.

> Let Rome in Tiber melt, and the wide arch
> Of the ranged empire fall! Here is my space,
> ... the nobleness of life
> Is to do thus, when such a mutual pair
> And such a twain can do't.
>
> I, i, 33–8

The parallel of macrocosm and microcosm was of course a commonplace to the Elizabethans: an example familiar to modern readers occurs in the last verse of John Donne's *The Sun Rising*.

> She's all States, and all Princes, I,
> Nothing else is.
> Princes do but play us; compared to this,
> All honour's mimic; all wealth alchemy.
> Thou sun art half as happy as we,
> In that the world's contracted thus;
> Thine age asks case, and since thy duties be
> To warm the world, that's done in warming us.
> Shine here to us and thou art everywhere;
> This bed thy centre is, these walls, thy sphere.

It is this juxtaposition of two worlds and Shakespeare's imaginative attitude towards it which unifies *Antony and Cleopatra* and which must decide its interpretation. It has already been suggested that Shakespeare refuses to endorse the values which are exemplified in Octavius Caesar.[1] In the private world of Antony and the queen, whose heart he rightly believed he had, those personal loyalties which Octavius denied are the ultimate values, though even the two lovers discovered their true nature very slowly. Their power, however, is enough to destroy Enobarbus who glimpsed and

---

[1] See above, pp. 66 f.; cf. also the rejection of Falstaff, pp. 59 ff.

betrayed them and who died before 'the cock crew twice', because after his treachery he had no reason to live:

> throw my heart
> Against the flint and hardness of my fault;
> ...O Antony,
> Nobler than my revolt is infamous,
> Forgive me in thine own particular;
> But let the world rank me in register
> A master-leaver and a fugitive.   IV, ix, 15–22

It is perhaps necessary first to scotch the misconception that Cleopatra had contemplated betraying Antony to Octavius. She is twice accused of this by Antony: once on his discovering her with Thyreus and once after the final defeat at Actium. Each time the accusation is made in the heat of violent passion; Shakespeare allows it no shred of supporting evidence and makes Antony forget it immediately his anger fades. Cleopatra certainly attempts to treat with Octavius both before and after Antony's death, and her purpose is made plain more than once: it is to ensure

> The circle of the Ptolemies for her heirs,   III, xii, 18

and she has a mistaken, but not unreasonable, faith in her ability to achieve it.

This is no betrayal of her lover, but until she has lost him she certainly has more concern for her own well-being than for his.

> *Antony*: I am dying, Egypt, dying; only
> I here importune death awhile, until
> Of many thousand kisses the poor last
> I lay upon thy lips.
> *Cleopatra*:   I dare not, dear,—
> Dear my lord, pardon,—I dare not,
> Lest I be taken: IV, xv, 18–23

On this follows the scene in which Antony is lifted up into the monument, the full implications of which in terms of the theatre need to be clearly visualised. The action involved should be almost as painful as the blinding of Gloucester. We know that Antony had been unarmed, and he had in effect laid bare his 'bosom to the

knife' as Antonio had done before him. He must have been covered
in blood and through eighteen lines of dragging speech and la-
boured action his mangled body is hoisted and manœuvred up the
ten or twelve feet to Cleopatra's arms. He is silent at first because he
is incapable of speech even as Thyreus was, after the flogging which
Antony had himself ordered, and he endures the agony to the end
without a word of protest. Only when he has drunk the cup of
wine is he able to make his last, ill-starred effort to safeguard her
after his death. His action does not surprise us for he has always
been shown as the more generous of the lovers and is therefore less
changed by the fire of suffering than she will be. For once she has
lost him a change begins in her too. She accepts the prospect of
death at once and arranges for the bringing of the asps before she is
captured or has been warned by Dolabella of Caesar's treachery.
She tries again to ensure her kingdom and her treasure for her sons,
but her thoughts are all on Antony, and her vivid descriptions of
the horrors of a Roman triumph are made to Charmian and Iras,
solely that she may be sure of their company on her last journey.
This motive is for them not for her, and her last speech is as purely
a love lyric as is Isolde's *Liebestod*.

There is a certain element of historical imagination in Shakespeare's Roman plays, for in one important respect he allows his
Romans a different code of conduct from that demanded from men
he thinks of as Christians. For these latter suicide is always a final
refusal of submission to the divine will, a mortal sin of either
arrogance or despair, but during the Renaissance men learned to
accept suicide in the classical world as no sin but rather a final
achievement of personal integrity. The end which Shakespeare
devises for this play shows that he recognises the final righteousness
of his queen of 'infinite variety' and intends his auditors to do the
same. The theatrical 'business' surrounding Cleopatra's death is of
extreme significance. The little group of the three women is the
centre of as big a crowd scene as the 'King's Men' could muster.
After the guard have come 'rustling in', there enters 'Caesar and all
his train, marching'. Thus the full might of the world's con-
querors faces the frail forces that have successfully defied and out-

witted them. The order for the final movement is given in Caesar's own voice:

Take up her bed.   v, ii, 359

This means that Cleopatra has died out on the apron-stage and must therefore necessarily be given a funeral procession. It is a final honour which she shares with Hamlet and Lear, who both fulfil their appointed roles in death, and with Coriolanus, who repented in time to save others though not himself and who, like Cleopatra, is given his last rites by his foes. It is important to remember that in the other play in which the end is concerned with the 'tragic loading' of a bed—*Othello*—the stage business is completely different.

Let it be hid:
Othello, v, ii, 365

commands Ludovico, thus proving that Desdemona's bed was set within the recess where it could be covered with a curtain. Othello, like Macbeth, is denied a funeral procession, and the significance of this is enforced by the realisation that Shakespeare sacrificed a moment of great dramatic effectiveness in order to have Macbeth killed off-stage. The processional ending, with its accompanying drum-beat—a Dead March is specifically allotted to the three men—is an infallible way to an audience's sympathy, and the fact that it is granted to Cleopatra and withheld from Othello is as clear a statement of the triumph of the one character as of the ultimate defeat of the other. Caesar's words end the play:

And then to Rome.
Antony and Cleopatra, v, ii, 368

The state has rolled like Juggernaut across the bodies of those who defied its claims and has exacted from them the utmost penalty. Nevertheless, the glory is theirs not Caesar's, and the new angle of vision is clear when the endings of earlier plays are remembered. The triumph of a young prince and the establishment of a kingdom's peace are no longer to the dramatist, as they once were, satisfactory symbols of achievement, for the old lion dying is here valued by his creator more highly than the lion's whelp who succceds him. In the synthesis finally achieved in the romances the dramatist is able to accept the positive goodness of each generation and to allow both old and young to share the moment of peace which his imagination achieves for them.

3. MEDIEVAL THOUGHT IN THE ROMANCES

Pericles; Cymbeline; A Winter's Tale; The Tempest

In spite of such changes as these, the threefold pattern of Sin and Judgment followed by Redemption, which was Shakespeare's medieval heritage and the earliest framework of his imaginative thought, persists to the end of his creative life. Only the conception of eternal damnation fades, to be succeeded by faith in the continual reawakening of the earth's fertility and of human love: those two aspects of Aphrodite called by the Italian neo-Platonists Venus Dione and Venus Umane. Although the brilliance of the theological symbolism fades and the imagery is increasingly sought from pre-Christian sources, yet there is no clear-cut break, and the old patterns are as clear in *The Tempest* as in *The Merchant of Venice*. As might be expected, they are of most significance in the presentation of the sin from which the action of the plays springs and of the punishment which follows it, and they must be traced and their importance admitted before any attempt is made to assess the new implications of the last plays. While Shakespeare increasingly shows man as a being fully integrated with the non-human universe and essentially akin to the vegetation which flowers and dies and drops new seeds to flower again in the spring, yet he never shows him as escaping from the imperatives of the Christian ethos.

It is soon obvious that the primary sin remains closely associated with *hubris* and the breach of degree. In *Pericles*, the first of the new series, the hero resembles Henry VI; his sin, in so far as it exists, is not any form of pride but a breach of degree—a failure to perform his function in the hierarchy. For although it is, in the main, the storms of circumstance which tear from Pericles his wife and daughter, yet he himself cannot be held free from all blame.

179

Pericles is one of a line of kings which, starting with Henry VI, includes King Lear. He leaves Helicanus to rule in Tyre when he is threatened by Antiochus, and although he does not abandon Marina as Leontes abandons Perdita, yet he leaves her to be nurtured by Cleon and Dionyza. These escapes from responsibility are not emphasised in the play as sins and might pass unnoticed were it not for the more strongly coloured figures to be seen elsewhere. Nevertheless, it is relevant that when Pericles is reunited to his wife he returns to his proper place in an ordered society and rules with Thaisa in Pentapolis, while his daughter and her husband inherit Tyre.

Cymbeline's sin is similarly negative in so far as he fails not in his kingly duties but in his parental ones. Imogen is cast out as Cordelia was, and it is Cymbeline's own action against Belarius, an act similar to Lear's against Kent, which causes the exile of his two sons also. In spite of the obvious parallels with *King Lear*, however, the play is in reality nearer to *Othello* for it is the inability of both Cymbeline and Posthumus to penetrate false-seeming which determines the course of the action. The queen, too often dismissed as a fairy-tale stepmother, is in fact a genuinely significant figure. She stands in the direct line of succession from Margaret of Anjou through Goneril, Regan and Lady Macbeth, so that Henry, Lear and Macbeth might all say with Cymbeline:

> Mine eyes
> Were not in fault, for she was beautiful;
> Mine ears, that heard her flattery; nor my heart,
> That thought her like her seeming.   v, v, 62–5

This blindness of Cymbeline is doubled by that of Posthumus, and here, though with much less psychological realism, the tragedy of Cyprus is acted again: goodness is unrecognised, the lying accusation is believed and the fury of physical jealousy leads to the planning of vengeance disguised to the avenger as justice. Unlike Othello, however, Posthumus finds humility in his suffering; he is even ready to forgive Imogen for unchastity, and he admits his own unworthiness to act as 'justicer'.

> You married ones,
> If each of you should take this course, how many
> Must murder wives much better than themselves
> For wrying but a little!...
> Gods! if you
> Should have ta'en vengeance on my faults, I never
> Had lived to put on this:...   v, i, 2–9

In his soliloquy of repentance Posthumus uses the word for ever charged with magic by Cordelia.

> Most welcome, bondage! for thou art a way,
> I think, to liberty;   v, iii, 3–4

and he continues with a disarming simplicity:

> Is't enough I am sorry?
> So children temporal fathers do appease;
> Gods are more full of mercy.   v, iii, 11–13

Shakespeare's answer to his question would undoubtedly have been 'No', but Posthumus does not only repent: he is also ready to render the *deeds of mercy*, for he pardons Iachimo:

> Kneel not to me:
> The power that I have on you is to spare you;
> The malice towards you to forgive you: live,
> And deal with others better.   v, vi, 417–20

In spite, however, of the genuineness of Posthumus' suffering and the beauty of his penitence, there is a flagrant evil in the play which is allowed to disappear all too easily; it has elicited neither the suffering nor the heroism which have regularly preceded the conquest of wickedness in the tragedies and is wafted out of existence in a way which carries scant conviction even in the glamour of the theatre.

Happily such slackening of tension is not more than temporary. In *A Winter's Tale* Shakespeare's treatment of *hubris* has all the fierceness of his earlier work, and *The Tempest* contains a full reflection of the Lucifer legend treated in the manner of a double fugue, with the assassinations of Prospero and Alonzo plotted by the Janus figure of Antonio-Sebastian and paralleled by the coun-

ter-subject of Caliban's rebellion. Now to the old material however is added a poignancy which springs from the new emphasis
on personal relationships. Those who suffer from the weakness of
Pericles and Cymbeline are not primarily their subjects but their
children, and it is the personal nature of Antonio's treachery which
makes the final challenge to Prospero's power to render mercy so
hard a one to face.

A Winter's Tale is the play in which the old and new motifs are
most powerfully combined. The friendship between Leontes and
Polixenes goes back to earliest childhood when they shared the
experiences which usually unite only blood brothers and sisters.

> We were as twinn'd lambs that did frisk i' the sun,
> And bleat the one at the other: what we changed
> Was innocence for innocence; we knew not
> The doctrine of ill-doing, nor dream'd
> That any did.   I, ii, 67–71

This is the bond which Leontes breaks when he orders Camillo
to kill Polixenes, and he breaks it, swayed—as were Othello and
Posthumus—by an unbearable physical jealousy which blinds him
to reality even while he thinks he alone is undeceived.

When we turn to Leontes' sin against Hermione the whole situation is at once intensified. The wrong itself is more horrible even
than Othello's because the relationship between the husband and
wife is more fully developed. Moreover, Leontes had none of the
excuses for his blindness which Shakespeare takes pains to emphasise in Othello's case. He is no 'extravagant and wheeling stranger',
recently wedded to a girl who must seem a being from another
planet. He is not rushed into hasty action by the scheming of a
demi-devil; on the contrary he takes time to pause, and all his
councillors urge him to reconsider an accusation which in their
eyes appears monstrous.

The climax of Leontes' *hubris* is where, in his individual distress,
he turns against the whole order of creation. The imprecations
of Lear and Macbeth against the 'germens . . . that make in-
grateful man' foreshadow this turning, but they are made in
the heat of passion and in general terms. Leontes' brutality to his

own pregnant wife sets an even keener edge on the attack. When Hermione's unborn baby becomes the focus of his virulence the whole process of gestation is made repulsive by his words. Against the gentle laughter of the women teasing Mamillius and accepting gladly the natural cycle of fertility ring his hideous gibes.

> *First Lady:*   Hark ye;
> The queen your mother rounds apace: we shall
> Present our services to a fine new prince
> One of these days; and then you'ld wanton with us
> If we would have you.
> *Second Lady:*   She is spread of late
> Into a goodly bulk; good time encounter her! . . .
> *Leontes:* Give me the boy: I am glad you did not nurse him:
> Though he does bear some signs of me, yet you
> Have too much blood in him.
> *Hermione:*   What is this? sport?
> *Leontes:* Bear the boy hence; he shall not come about her;
> Away with him! and let her sport herself
> With that she's big with; for 'tis Polixenes
> Has made thee swell thus.   II, i, 15–62

In his crazy faith in his own darkened vision he can say:

>   How blest am I
> In my just censure, in my true opinion!
> Alack, for lesser knowledge! how accursed
> In being so blest! There may be in the cup
> A spider steep'd, and one may drink, depart,
> And yet partake no venom, for his knowledge
> Is not infected: but if one present
> The abhorr'd ingredient to his eye, make known
> How he hath drunk, he cracks his gorge, his sides,
> With violent hefts. I have drunk and seen the spider.   II, i, 36–45

To Leontes, love and life have become the poisonous spider, nothing more.

The casting-out of the new-born baby is another direct attack on the future, on the continuity of life, but Perdita fortunately depends not on her royal father nor on her 'own protection and favour of the climate' (II, iii, 178–9), but on the kindness of a simple old shepherd, for whom the claims of humanity overrule both danger and the social values which had caused Leontes' cruelty:

what have we here? Mercy on's, a barne;... A pretty one; a very pretty one: sure, some 'scape: though I am not bookish, yet I can read waiting-gentlewoman in the 'scape. This has been some stair-work, some trunk-work, some behind-door-work: they were warmer that got this than the poor thing is here. I'll take it up for pity.   III, iii, 70–8

Finally, Leontes' rebellion against God becomes explicit, for he openly repudiates the word from Delphos:

> There is no truth at all i' the oracle:
> The sessions shall proceed: this is mere falsehood.
>
> III, ii, 141–2

The suffering which inevitably follows from this defiance is both Leontes' punishment and his purgation.

The first half of the play has much to do with the contrast between divine law and the human justice which Hermione declares to be 'rigour and not law' and against which Antigonus has warned the king:

> Be certain what you do, sir, lest your justice
> Prove violence.   II, i, 127–8

Leontes makes great protestation that they are both wrong:

> Let us be clear'd
> Of being tyrannous, since we so openly
> Proceed in justice, which shall have due course,
> Even to the guilt or the purgation.   III, ii, 4–7

But Hermione can show that such claims are unwarranted even by the common standards of civilised society; she appeals therefore to the oracle, and Shakespeare has been at pains to charge the word with associations diametrically opposed to the hurly-burly and passions of Leontes' all too human court. The idyllic duet between the two messengers describing the delivering of the divine revelation is one of those moments when the action of a play is deliberately stilled so that the full imaginative value of the lines may impose themselves on the ear:

Cleomenes: The climate's delicate, the air most sweet,
Fertile the isle, the temple much surpassing
The common praise it bears.
Dion: I shall report,
For most it caught me, the celestial habits,
Methinks I so should term them, and the reverence
Of the grave wearers. O, the sacrifice!
How ceremonious, solemn and unearthly
It was i' the offering!
Cleomenes: But of all the burst
And the ear-deafening voice o' the oracle,
Kin to Jove's thunder, so surprised my sense,
That I was nothing.   III, i, 1–11

Human justice proves to be no more than the expression of human arrogance and folly, but from the serene beauty of Delphos come, in the fullness of time, mercy and forgiveness.

Although it is Prospero himself who commits the fault that is the starting-point of *The Tempest* and, by casting the government upon his brother, first 'takes degree away' in Milan, it is the active sin of rebellion which dominates the play's structure. The two Neapolitan brothers are both the tools of that more sinister figure Antonio; Sebastian presumably speaks for both of them when he says:

to ebb
Hereditary sloth instructs me,   *The Tempest*, II, i, 222–3

and inertia and circumstances together save him from his purposed fratricide. Alonzo also sinned in part through lethargy. He appears to have taken 'suggestion as a cat laps milk'. His fault is treachery against an ally, followed by connivance at murder. His penalty is severe, for he believes that he has lost his only son and heir, and his suffering is real. Moreover, he accepts it as just and recognises that the evil he committed was something against the natural order of the universe, referring to it as 'monstrous'[1] and

---

[1] It is possible to consider that the word refers to the means by which his guilt is revealed and brought home to him, but on the whole the above reading seems preferable.

genuinely desiring to make restitution by sacrificing himself if it
were possible:

> O, it is monstrous, monstrous!
> Methought the billows spoke and told me of it;
> The winds did sing it to me, and the thunder,
> That deep and dreadful organ-pipe, pronounced
> The name of Prosper: it did bass my trespass.
> Therefore my son i' the ooze is bedded, and
> I'll seek him deeper than e'er plummet sounded.
> And with him there lie mudded.   III, iii, 95–102

One may suppose that it is by one of Gonzalo's many faithful services that he lives to be saved by his 'sea-sorrow', even as Prospero
was by his.

Antonio is a more interesting figure: his first sin is a dual one, for
it is against Prospero who is both his king and his brother, and it is
the second aspect which is stressed and which Prospero finds it so
hard to pardon. Laertes and Hamlet as well as Edgar and Edmund
exchanged forgiveness in the hour of death, but though these men
have wronged or even killed each other in the excitement of combat, they have not been hurt as Prospero was hurt. In the earlier
plays only women have pardoned the kind of personal outrage that
Prospero has endured; Cordelia, Desdemona, Imogen and Hermione do so in a love which makes forgiveness appear an irrele-
vance; Isabella, without personal love to help her, only after a
struggle as great as Prospero's own. Like Isabella, Prospero forgives the enemy before he repents, but, unlike Angelo, Antonio is
not moved by forgiveness to repentance. There is more than a
trace of Macbeth in the sterility of his evil. He confederated with
Naples because 'so dry he was for sway', and when he is compared
to a plant it is to a parasite; for Prospero he is:

> The ivy which had hid my princely trunk,
> And suck'd my verdure out on't.   I, ii, 86–7

Antonio's second sin is a faint echo of his first. Alonzo is neither
his king nor his brother; he is merely a political inconvenience,
and the dramatic purpose of the plot against him is to show that

Antonio has not changed. He is willing to use the old weapons to remove a trivial obstacle in his upward path—the tribute due to Naples. Shakespeare ensures that Prospero has plenty to think of when he says:

> For you, most wicked sir, whom to call brother
> Would even infect my mouth, I do forgive
> Thy rankest fault,—all of them. v, i, 130–2

A recognition of the significance of this new focus, this closing-in, as it were, of the field of man's sin, is essential for a clear appreciation of Shakespeare's development as a poet. It is a long road from *Henry VI* to *The Tempest*, and as he travelled it Shakespeare trusted the clues given him by the great religio-political tradition into which he had been born. He made himself, and demanded from his audience, a full response to the figure of the king—'the deputy elected by the Lord'—and to the figure beyond him of that Lord himself. In the plays just considered, however, although he continues to show men to be as aggressive, as violent and as self-seeking as ever, their sin is less the sin of Adam than the sin of Cain: it is not against their God but against their fellow-men, and it is from the love and mercy of their fellow-men, and not from the final judgment of a divine Saviour, that their redemption must come, if it is to come at all.

CHAPTER VII

THE NEW IMAGERY
AND THE FINAL SYNTHESIS

A Winter's Tale; Pericles; Cymbeline; The Tempest; King John;
Twelfth Night; Antony and Cleopatra; Romeo and Juliet

The preceding analysis has, it is hoped, demonstrated that while the final plays include much that is traditional in Shakespeare's work, the sources of their dynamism must also be sought in new country. The tap-root of the dramatist's imagination appears to be feeling its way towards deeper strata of association, until at last the familiar struggle between justice and mercy is reflected afresh in the imagery of a pagan world, and a new—or it may be a more ancient —conclusion is voiced.

The Christian Church, in spite of its great seasonal festivals, has never made extensive use of seasonal imagery, and in as far as it does so its central symbol is the child born in mid-winter—'a thing of pity'—rather than the man risen in the spring.[1] But although such material had only a small place in Christian thought and there-fore in medieval written drama, it had of course existed in dramatic or semi-dramatic form from time immemorial—as indeed it still exists today in plays of St George and of the Hobby-Horse, the Revesby Sword Play, the Furry Dance of Helston and countless other local celebrations. The May games, already noticed in con-nection with the symbol of Birnam Wood, made an underground connection with the figure of Robin Hood, and probably the earliest secular written drama in English is the fragment concerning Robin Hood and the Sheriff of Nottingham.[2] Robin and Maid Marian are associated with the king and queen of the May by the version of *Robin Hood and the Potter*, printed in 1560 under the

---

[1] The medieval songs of winter are typically Christian carols, but those of spring are mostly secular love-songs.
[2] *Collections* I, 2, Malone Society Reprint (1908).

rubric: 'Here beginnethe the plays of Robin Hoode, verye proper to be played in May Games.'[1] Much similar material is used dramatically in *Summer's Last Will and Testament*.[2] Other channels leading from pre-Christian springs of imagery were the Romances, which contributed many folk-traditions to drama. Well-known examples occur in *Clyomon and Clamides* with its setting of 'a forest of marvels',[3] while *The Rare Triumphs of Love and Fortune*[4] and *Mucedorus*[5] also contain young lovers who are sheltered in some remote place and finally emerge from their leafy refuge to bring to their elders a happy ending. Bomelio on his first glimpse of Fidelia exclaims:

> thou nymph or lady fair,
> Or else thou goddess of the grove, what mak'st thee to repair
> To this unhaunted place?
>
> *Rare Triumphs*, III

In the epilogue Venus can justly assert:

> Thus everything united is by love.
> Now gods and men are reconciled again. *Ibid.*, v

In Shakespeare's romances the source of salvation is usually a dual figure, male and female: Florizel and Perdita dance together at the Whitsun Pastorals dressed as king and queen of the May; nevertheless, the imaginative emphasis is always placed on the woman. This is scarcely surprising when it is remembered with what force the earlier heroines are projected. Juliet, Portia and Rosalind all overshadow their lovers and are the principal vessels of regenerative power in the plays in which they move. Nevertheless, there is a difference between them and the heroines of the romances. Not only do these latter become increasingly non-naturalistic in conception, but in the last plays revival is no longer shown in the simple terms of natural procreation: their heroines bring renewed life not only to their lovers but also to an older and failing generation. They are essentially virgin goddesses of spring, renewing a fading world.

---

[1] *Collections* I, i, Malone Society Reprint. Dated *c.* 1475 by Greg.
[2] Dodsley, *Old English Plays*, vol. VII. [3] Malone Society Reprint (1913).
[4] Dodsley, *Old English Plays*, vol. VI. [5] *Ibid.*, vol. VII.

Florizel: These your unusual weeds to each part of you
Do give a life: no shepherdess, but Flora
Peering in April's front.

A Winter's Tale, IV, iv, 1–3

Prospero's adjurations to Ferdinand not to anticipate the leading of 'Hymen's lamps' are distasteful at the level of naturalism, but through their wedding masque the love of Ferdinand and Miranda is universalised in a paean to natural fertility. Miranda's maidenhead is not simply her own or even her contracted husband's; it is the earth's and belongs to its peoples to whom she will bring in due course the new spring. In these plays the winter–spring imagery appears like a huge shadow thrown by the events of the story of justice and mercy which the play tells. In each case the forgiveness of the sinner is associated with the emergence of a primeval world of natural beauty, youth and fertile love. The redemption is seen as a renewed life which must be the gift of youth to age, if age is to receive it at all. It includes both a rediscovery of a pre-lapsarian Eden and a return from it to the world of men. Thus the Christian message is combined with the even older version of the battle between life and death. The pattern is adumbrated in many of Shakespeare's earlier plays. We must remember Cordelia and even Cleopatra as well as Birnam Wood. In the romances, however, Shakespeare develops more fully his own peculiar version of his archetype. It becomes both softened and humanised, and the old are allowed for one golden moment to share in the new life.

The Christian concept of mercy is never abandoned; it is indeed restated and developed, but it is conflated with another: the necessary acceptance of the recurring life-cycle of man as a part of nature. A willing submission to the human condition is the hall-mark of these magical plays, which yet contain no mitigation of the facts of experience, for in them evil is as actual as goodness. They are as 'moral' as a morality, yet they suggest no finality whether of salvation or damnation. Life continues, and its perpetual renewal is accepted while the conception of perpetual damnation is refused. It is the marriage of the figures of natural magic with the accumulated values of the Christian *ethos* which gives to the last plays their extraordinary potency.

Of all the 'shapes' into which the poet's pen turns these 'forms of things unknown', the most important is that of the 'bringers-in' of spring. Their advent is always tinged with mystery. Like that of Arthur Pendragon their birth is, not indeed miraculous—that would be too far removed from the drama's secular convention—but yet in some way abnormal. Macduff, who shares the rescue of Scotland with Malcolm, 'was from his mother's womb untimely ripped', and Marina and Perdita were both born prematurely amid unusual suffering. Thaisa, as we are told by Gower:

> Does fall in travail with her fear;
>
> *Pericles*, III, Prologue, 52

and her 'terrible childbed' appears to result in her death. Of Hermione Emilia reports:

> on her frights and griefs,
> Which never tender lady hath borne greater,
> She is something before her time deliver'd.
>
> *A Winter's Tale*, II, ii, 23–5

Posthumus shares Macduff's distinction:

> *Mother*: Lucina lent me not her aid,
> But took me in my throes;
> That from me was Posthumus ript,
> Came crying 'mongst his foes,
> A thing of pity!
>
> *Cymbeline*, V, iv, 43–7

This case is slightly ambiguous, for Cymbeline's own children are the principal source of regeneration; nevertheless, Posthumus Leonatus is a princely figure, who helps to free his country from an alien tyranny. He is also a sinner and a victim of falseseeming, but he becomes the consort of Imogen and therefore plays the role more clearly developed later by Florizel and Ferdinand. It is of interest that this element of mystery concerning a hero's birth appears first in Macbeth, which is so closely related by its fertility imagery and symbolism to the thought of the last plays.[1]

In the romances the symbols of the mysterious birth and of the advent by water join in a concept of which the presentations most familiar today are probably found in the paintings of Botticelli. The naked girl, soon to be clad in the red, flower-strewn cloak, of the *Birth of Venus* and the benign figure central to the *Primavera* have both been related by Professor Edgar Wind[2] to the neo-Platonism —familiar to Spenser, and at least accessible to Shakespeare—in which the Venus Urania, or Divine Love, becomes the Venus Dione who enters the natural world to ensure its fertility and continuance. The simplest and perhaps most beautiful of such epiphanies is in *Pericles*. Marina does not indeed come, as do the other daughters, directly from the Eden-innocence of our first world, where

> the leaves were full of children
> Hidden excitedly, containing laughter.[3]

But she appears with her arms full of spring flowers and goes on to spread the perfumed sweetness of her own enchantments around her, even in the brothel of Mitylene. The Quarto of 1609 makes the visual symbol certain by its stage direction.

Enter MARINA, *with a basket of flowers*

> *Marina*: No, I will rob Tellus of her weed,
>   To strew thy green with flowers: the yellows, blues,
>   The purple violets, and marigolds,
>   Shall as a carpet hang upon thy grave,
>   While summer-days do last.   IV, i, 14–18

This is her first appearance on the stage but as a baby she was blown on to the shores of middle-earth from the sea just as was Venus Dione herself. To Leonine she describes her birth:

> *Marina*: My father, as nurse said, did never fear,
>   But cried 'Good seamen!' to the sailors, galling
>   His kingly hands, haling ropes;

---

[1] There are folk-traditions in England concerning the magical powers of a posthumous but none, that this writer has discovered, of a premature, child.

[2] *Pagan Mysteries in the Renaissance* (1958).   [3] T. S. Eliot, *Burnt Norton*.

> And, clasping to the mast, endured a sea
> That almost burst the deck.
> *Leonine*: When was this?
> *Marina*: When I was born.   IV, i, 53–9

When Pericles recognises her he says:

> O, come hither,
> Thou that beget'st him that did thee beget;
> Thou that wast born at sea, buried at Tarsus,
> And found at sea again!   v, i, 196–9

Water, so often the image of estrangement and calamity, is also the bringer of life to the desiccated wintry land of the aged 'Fisher King', so that with Marina's return the Chain of Being runs again unbroken from earth to heaven.

> *Pericles*:   But, what music?
> *Helicanus*: My lord, I hear none.
> *Pericles*: None!
> The music of the spheres! List my Marina....
> Most heavenly music!   v, i, 228–34

This music is indeed

> no mortal business, nor no sound
> That the earth owes . . .
>
> *The Tempest*, I, ii, 406–7

In the three plays following *Pericles* the tentative image of Marina's basket of flowers is developed into the garden world in which the figures of spring are nurtured until the time for their blossoming is come. In *Cymbeline* Belarius and the two princes are cut off from society, living in isolation and concerned with no demands beyond their personal needs. Theirs is the imaginary world of a fairy tale.

In *A Winter's Tale* the image is a more realistic one; we see a genuine rustic society, lively enough, although unable to protect its members from the hazards of the encroaching world or to offer them its opportunities. In *The Tempest* the island is a poet's dream, neither more nor less. But all three plays have answered in the affirmative T. S. Eliot's question:

> Into our first world
> Shall we follow the deception of the thrush?[1]

They recreate the lost Age of Innocence, the imagined garden, whether of Eden or of the Hesperides or, more simply, the real though fragile security created by the loving parent for the beloved child.

In *Cymbeline* and *A Winter's Tale* there are made explicit both the beauty of such a world and its insufficiency. Guiderius and Arviragus can grow up but not rest content in it.

> *Guiderius*:   Haply this life is best,
>   If quiet life be best; sweeter to you
>   That have a sharper known...
> 											but unto us it is
>   A cell of ignorance.   *Cymbeline*, III, iii, 29–33

Although Belarius paints feelingly the evil and puerilities of the life at court from which he has withdrawn, yet Arviragus knows that in spite of its 'complexities of mire or blood',[2] it is a more truly human society than theirs, in which man approximates to the simplicity of the beasts. He asks Belarius:

> 								What should we speak of
>   When we are old as you? when we shall hear
>   The rain and wind beat dark December, how,
>   In this our pinching cave, shall we discourse
>   The freezing hours away? We have seen nothing;
>   We are beastly, subtle as the fox for prey,
>   Like warlike as the wolf for what we eat.   III, iii, 35–41

The young princes are already outgrowing their nursery and beginning,

>   In simple and low things to prince it much
>   Beyond the trick of others.   III, iii, 85–6

Perdita resembles them in this: she is indeed 'a queen of curds and cream'. These young people could each of them say:

>   Fair seed time had my soul, and I grew up
>   Fostered alike by beauty and by fear.[3]

---

[1] T. S. Eliot, *Burnt Norton*.   [2] W. B. Yeats, *Byzantium*.   [3] Wordsworth, *Prelude* I.

Unlike Wordsworth, however, Shakespeare never implies that man is able to attain his full stature in such a world. Perdita does not accept this limitation at first, and in her love of what she thinks is natural she refuses to grow streaked gillyvors, because, as she declares:

> I have heard it said
> There is an art which in their piedness shares
> With great creating nature.
>
> *A Winter's Tale*, iv, iv, 86–8

Polixenes in this section of the play is cast in an unpleasing role, and all our sympathy moves instinctively to Perdita; nevertheless it is impossible to confute his plea that man's true nature is only to be found by transcending what appears to him, in his early childish ignorance, to be natural.

> *Polixenes*: Yet nature is made better by no mean
> But nature makes that mean; so, over that art
> Which you say adds to nature, is an art
> That nature makes. . . .   iv, iv, 89–92

Man is not created to be a 'bare, forked animal' and, as Lear learned at last, must find himself not in stripping off the sophistication of his soiled garments but in receiving and wearing fresh ones. Perdita herself knew well enough that the apparent security and sufficiency of the garden in which she was living was a fragile defence against the evil of the world. She says to her lover:

> Even now I tremble
> To think your father, by some accident,
> Should pass this way as you did: . . .
> Your resolution cannot hold, when 'tis
> Opposed, as it must be, by the power of the king:
> One of these two must be necessities,
> Which then will speak, that you must change this purpose,
> Or I my life.   iv, iv, 18–39

Although she did not know it, the evil was already within her Arcadia, and its humble framework was about to topple. She soon finds reason to say:

this dream of mine,—
Being now awake, I'll queen it no inch farther,
But milk my ewes and weep.   IV, iv, 458–60

But just as she accepted what she understood of the demands of her sheltered world, so she was ready to face the dangers of the fuller life beyond it and, when the time came, to seek it with her lover.

In *The Tempest*, the island-Eden, where all evil is safely controlled by Prospero's magic and where even Venus may not land without his permission, has become the scene of almost the entire play, but the other world is never forgotten. In spite of his powers Prospero is not presented to us as a god. As Professor C. S. Lewis[1] has demonstrated, he is someone who has learnt to practise white magic with success. And since he is a man, and a sinful man, it is right as well as inevitable that he should disappear and be succeeded by youth. The greatness of Prospero lies in his conscious participation in his own supplanting, in his holding of his supplanters to be his 'dear beloveds' and in his willing submission to the ineluctable passage of time.

I'll break my staff,
Bury it certain fathoms in the earth,
And deeper than did ever plummet sound,
I'll drown my book.   v, i, 54–7

We are such stuff
As dreams are made on, and our little life
Is rounded with a sleep.   IV, i, 156–8

The price of such a final redemption is not paid only by the sinner. In each of the four romances it involves an innocent person who suffers for the sin of another and accepts this suffering so that it becomes the vicarious sacrifice of a willing victim. This victim may not coincide with the youthful life-bringer, but the connection between them is sometimes so close that they appear as aspects of the same figure. Clear examples are Hermione, the mother of Perdita, and Thaisa, the mother of Marina. Hermione both invokes and submits to the message from Delphos, bearing the con-

[1] *Oxford History of Literature*, vol. III, ed. by F. P. Wilson and B. Dobrée (1954).

sequences of Leontes' guilt for sixteen years, and her expiation involves a form of death from which she at last returns to him. A comparison of their roles makes plain that of Thaisa, who 'dies' and is cast, Jonah-like, into the sea.

> *Pericles:*   nor have I time
> To give thee hallow'd to thy grave, but straight
> Must cast thee, scarcely coffin'd, in the ooze;
> Where, for a monument upon thy bones,
> And e'er-remaining lamps, the belching whale
> And humming water must o'erwhelm thy corpse,
> Lying with simple shells.   III, i, 59–65

The content of the scene between Hermione and Leontes in Paulina's chapel is divided in *Pericles*. Thaisa revives among strangers in an unknown land:

> *Cerimon:*   see how she gins to blow
> Into life's flower again!...
>   Live,
> And make us weep to hear your fate, fair creature,
> Rare as you seem to be.
> *Thaisa:*   O dear Diana,
> Where am I? Where's my lord? What world is this?
>   III, ii, 95–106

Her return to her husband takes place in Diana's temple and, like Hermione's in Paulina's chapel, is delayed for many lonely years. Then she recovers both husband and child.

> *Thaisa:*   O, my lord,
> Are you not Pericles? Like him you spake,
> Like him you are: did you not name a tempest,
> A birth, and death?
> *Pericles:* ...you gods... you shall do well,
> That on the touching of her lips I may
> Melt and no more be seen. O, come, be buried
> A second time within these arms...
> Look, who kneels here! Flesh of thy flesh, Thaisa;
> Thy burden at the sea, and call'd Marina
> For she was yielded there.
> *Thaisa:*   Blest, and mine own!   V, iii, 31–48

Imogen also, driven into the wilderness by her husband, 'dies' and
is buried.

> *Arviragus*:   The bird is dead
> That we have made so much on...
>
>   With fairest flowers
> While summer lasts and I live here, Fidele,
> I'll sweeten thy sad grave.
>
> *Cymbeline*, IV, ii, 197–8, 218–20

She endures a second death, when the man for whom she suffers
himself strikes her without recognising her.

> *Pisanio*:   O, gentlemen, help!
> Mine and your mistress! O, my lord Posthumus!
> You ne'er kill'd Imogen till now...   V, v, 229–31

The most fully developed of these figures is that of Hermione
because she is the one who consciously fulfils the demands of the
gods, seeking and winning the power to do so for the sake of her
husband. It is she and Paulina who understand the 'secret purposes'
of God whereas Leontes does not. Paulina says to the councillors:

> Is't not the tenour of his oracle,
> That King Leontes shall not have an heir
> Till his lost child be found? which that it shall,
> Is all as monstrous to our human reason
> As my Antigonus to break his grave
> And come again to me:...
>
>   'Tis your counsel
> My lord should to the heavens be contrary,
> Oppose against their wills.   V, i, 38–46

The reason for Hermione's withdrawal is clear from the oracle:

> and the king shall live without an heir, if that which is lost be not found.
>
>   III, ii, 136–7

There must be no more children: Hermione has learnt wisdom in
her humiliation. As she foresaw:

>   ...this action I now go on,
> Is for my better grace.   II, i, 121–2

It is in her power to ensure Leontes' submission to the oracle, and she does ensure it by her absence. Leontes' long purgation is a very different matter from the all too easy repentance of Posthumus, and it is only when he has 'perform'd a saint-like sorrow' that the seas bring back his lost child to him.

> One that gives out himself Prince Florizel,
> Son of Polixenes, with his princess, she
> The fairest I have yet beheld, desires access
> To your high presence.   v, i, 85–8

And now Paulina can call Leontes' Alcestis back from the shades in which she has lingered to bring her husband life.

> 'Tis time; descend; be stone no more; approach;
> Strike all that look upon with marvel. Come,
> I'll fill your grave up; stir, nay come away,
> Bequeath to death your numbness, for from him
> Dear life redeems you....
>   Turn, good lady;
> Our Perdita is found.   v, iii, 99–121

Hermione might well have said to Leontes: 'I love your majesty, according to my bond; nor more nor less', and it is exactly such love which, by enduring through the long years, at last ensures his redemption.

In *The Tempest* the role of substitute victim is played by Ferdinand, the lover of Miranda and her male counterpart, who suffers for the sin of his father and returns to him after a 'death' by drowning which Alonzo knows should have been his own:

> I wish
> Myself were mudded in that oozy bed
> Where my son lies.   v, i, 150–2

It is possible that Shakespeare's original intention was to allow Antonio to undergo the experiences that would have led him also at last to repentance. Such a supposition would explain that faint ghost of the son whom Ferdinand believes drowned:

> The Duke of Milan
> And his brave son being twain.   I, ii, 437–8

Perhaps Shakespeare had originally imagined one more Holy Innocent. If this ever were his intention, however, he changed it and put Antonio to a different purpose. Forgiveness after repentance, and especially after suffering which has changed and purified the offender, is readily acceptable to the human imagination: forgiveness of the unrepentant man is not. Antonio of Venice with his enigmatic melancholy is a character given a slightly more complex reality than is necessary for his role in the plot, and perhaps he grew thus in Shakespeare's mind because it is he who faces Shylock after Portia's challenge:

> What mercy can you render him, Antonio?   IV, i, 79

Under the somewhat—to us—distasteful complications of the inheritance and the enforced baptism, Antonio does in effect offer Shylock the complete and undeserved forgiveness which Prospero finally offers Antonio of Milan. They each forgive, not only those 'being penitent', but also the silent, unbending figure of the man who is not. Antonio forgives his open enemy but Prospero, after a harder struggle, the brother whom he had loved and trusted.

Of all the saviour figures Cordelia remains the clearest reflexion in the terms of Shakespeare's drama of the Christ whose crucifixion had been directly dramatised in the miracle plays. She dies because she has bought her father life. Her death is neither more nor less than the rest, and it is actual not symbolic because the play is written in the convention of tragedy, not that of romance. In spite of the underlying religious imagery there is no evidence that Shakespeare meant his work to be interpreted anagogically. It is indeed such delicate ambivalences as that of Lear asking and accepting forgiveness in a world where the distinction between divine and human love is obliterated, which reveal not only his deepest insight but his most subtle methods. The gifts of redemption, of love and of life are offered within the limitations of mortality by one human being to another, though always with the divine blessing implied or explicit.

> *Pericles*: Now do I long to hear how you were found;
> How possibly preserved; and who to thank,

Besides the gods, for this great miracle.
Thaisa: Lord Cerimon, my lord; this man,
Through whom the gods have shown their power,

Pericles, v, iii, 56–60

The harsh cry of Rightwyseness

As he has brewed, let him drink.

Castle of Perseverance

has been given a new application: it is the seeds of human love
which are now shown bearing fruit of like nature to themselves.

But Shakespeare's treatment of the theme of mercy which brings
renewed life was not finished when he had pictured a man forgiven by others and forgiving them in turn, for a man must become reconciled not only to his enemies but to himself. The sub-
stance of the scene between Pericles and Marina is so exquisite in its
fragility that if it were by any other writer one might refrain from
touching it, but as it is we may hazard a comment. Surely Pericles
meets and recognises at Mytilene not only his daughter but a part of
himself. At Tarsus Pericles as a complete individual ceased to be.
We have seen how Helicanus described him to Lysimachus and
explained that:

...the main grief springs from the loss
Of a beloved daughter and a wife.   v, i, 29–30

Pericles has failed twice; he could not save his wife from the storm
nor his daughter from her enemies. After his first failure we have
seen how he abandoned his own fatherhood as well as his child
and later reaped the fruits of his 'great refusal'. Self-knowledge
was unbearable, and it was Pericles who 'died' at Tarsus, not
Marina.

This was a goodly person,
Till the disaster that, one mortal night,
Drove him to this.   v, i, 36–8

When at last he can take the slender white figure of Marina into his
arms he is reunited with a part of his own soul, which he finds 'is not
dead at Tarsus as she should have been'. It is after this reunion that
he hears 'the music of the spheres'. In *King John* the matter-of-fact

First Citizen of Angiers spoke words which are curiously relevant:

> He is the half part of a blessed man,
> Left to be finished by such as she;
> And she a fair divided excellence,
> Whose fulness of perfection lies in him.   II, i, 437–40

Twelfth Night has foretold the joy of the recovery of lost love together with the lost self:

> *Sebastian*:   I had a sister,
> Whom the blind waves and surges have devour'd.
> Of charity, what kin are you to me?...
> Were you a woman, as the rest goes even,
> I should my tears let fall upon your cheek,
> And say 'Thrice-welcome, drowned Viola!'...
> *Viola*: If nothing lets to make us happy both
> But this my masculine usurp'd attire,
> Do not embrace me till each circumstance
> Of place, time, fortune, do cohere and jump
> That I am Viola.   v, i, 235–60

When the identical figures of Viola and Sebastian do at last melt together, they are a visible symbol of one complete personality, with male and female elements integrated at last and ready, as Pericles was, to hear 'the music of the spheres'.

This inward healing of the divided mind is the source from which wells up some of the almost overwhelming emotion of the scene of fantasy in Paulina's gallery in *A Winter's Tale*. Although Leontes has 'perform'd a saint-like sorrow', he has still not forgiven himself after sixteen years of penitence:

> Whilst I remember
> Her and her virtues, I cannot forget
> My blemishes in them.   v, i, 6–8

When he sees the 'statue' his first words are:

> Chide me, dear stone, that I may say indeed
> Thou art Hermione; or rather, thou art she
> In thy not chiding,...
>   O royal piece,

> There's magic in thy majesty, which has
> My evils conjured to remembrance.   v, iii, 24–40

It is the touch of the living Hermione which at last wins him from a sterile self-hatred to a glad acceptance of life once more:

> O, she's warm!
> If this be magic, let it be an art
> Lawful as eating,   v, iii, 109–11

These are hard matters for a wedding masque, but in *The Tempest* Shakespeare has twined them among the most fantastic and comical threads of his fabric, where they gleam bright to the seeing eye even if they are sometimes unnoticed. Caliban and Ariel are certainly a magician's servants, but they were created by a man who knew *magia* from the outside only, and they must draw at least a part of their glowing vitality from that man's direct experience of life. One of their sources appears to have been their creator's vision of man's divided mind. Urging Stephano against Prospero Caliban says:

> Remember
> First to possess his books; for without them
> He's but a sot, as I am.   III, ii, 99–101

Prospero would have agreed with him, for later he makes a strange admission—in words surely a little too solemn for their overt occasion:

> this thing of darkness I
> Acknowledge mine.   v, i, 275–6

The part of man's nature externalised in Caliban is an essential of life within the limitations of the human condition.

> ... As 'tis,
> We cannot miss him: I, ii, 310–11

says Prospero to Miranda. Caliban performs exactly the same tasks for his first master as he does for Stephano. Man, however powerful his mind, requires logs for warmth, fresh springs for drink and fruits of the earth for food, and his body is equipped to supply these needs. But Caliban is not only earthbound and a symbol of man's bodily faculties; he is also wicked. His gloating over Prospero's murder is truly repulsive and befitting only 'a thing most brutish':

> 'tis a custom with him,
> I' th' afternoon to sleep: there thou mayst brain him,
> Having first seized his books, or with a log
> Batter his skull, or paunch him with a stake,
> Or cut his wezand with thy knife.   III, ii, 95–9

Miranda, like Leontes and Polixenes in their boyhood, can live within her garden-island and 'know not the doctrine of ill-doing nor dream that any did', but evil lurks in all such gardens, and men have never conceived an Eden without a serpent. Shakespeare appears to have imagined the child living for a time untouched by the threat, for Prospero saves Miranda from Caliban, and Polixenes believed that:

> Had we pursued that life,
> And our weak spirits ne'er been higher rear'd
> With stronger blood, we should have answer'd heaven
> Boldly 'not guilty'.
> A Winter's Tale, I, ii, 71–4

But every mature man and woman has of necessity been reared with 'stronger blood' and has 'slipped since'; Prospero is no native of the Island but of Milan. The evil within the garden is within him also; he is in some measure identified with the enemy whom he strives to subdue and who is

> deservedly confined into this rock,
> Who hadst deserved more than a prison.
> The Tempest, I, ii, 361–2

If Prospero is to forgive himself, he must forgive Caliban, and it is the identification of Caliban with a part of himself that gives poignancy to the final exchange between Prospero and his servant-monster:

> Prospero: Go, sirrah, to my cell;
>   …as you look
> To have my pardon, trim it handsomely.
> Caliban: Ay, that I will; and I'll be wise hereafter
> And seek for grace. What a thrice-double ass

> Was I, to take this drunkard for a god
> And worship this dull fool!   v, i, 291–7

The final reconciliation of the divided selves is here presented as attained only as a grace, a gift from without, received after long search.

The theological overtones are very clear in *The Tempest* because of the close juxtaposition of the words *grace* and *gods*—a juxtaposition merely fortuitous when taken in the context of plot or character, but significant in the realm of ideas. We must remember, however, that Shakespeare elsewhere uses *grace* in a different context. It is of the dead Cleopatra that he says:

> she looks like sleep,
> As she would catch another Antony
> In her strong toil of grace.   v, ii, 349–51

The reality of Cleopatra's 'grace' is made clear by the false grace of Octavius, which has just been emphasised. So completely did Antony lose his judgment in Egypt that his dying advice to Cleopatra was to trust only Proculeius, the very man who does in fact betray her, and it is this man who blasphemously misapplies the word 'grace' to his master.

> *Proculeius*: Make your full reference freely to my lord,
> Who is so full of grace, that it flows over
> On all that need: let me report to him
> Your sweet dependency; and you shall find
> A conqueror that will pray in aid for kindness,
> When he for grace is kneel'd to.   v, ii, 23–8

Cleopatra continues the religious imagery, for she replies:

> I hourly learn
> A doctrine of obedience;   v, ii, 30–1

but here she is playing a part, and when Octavius enters and promises her 'care and pity', she immediately recognises the falsity of this apparent 'grace'.

> He words me, girls, he words me, that I should not
> Be noble to myself.   v, ii, 191–2

and Dolabella re-enters to confirm her fears. When Cleopatra is 'again for Cydnus, to meet Mark Antony', she is no longer tempting her lover to the various deceptions of either Rome or Egypt. At last she can offer him a love which accepts the obligation of the great 'bond of nature', submission to which can transform both the fancy which is 'engender'd in the eyes'[1] and the lust which is an 'expense of spirit in a waste of shame',[2] to a truly human love:

> husband, I come:
> Now to that name my courage prove my title!
> I am fire and air; my other elements
> I give to baser life.   v, ii, 290–3

It is in Cleopatra's description of her dream that Shakespeare makes his most specific statement of the nature and value of the human love which in this play fulfils, for the characters who experience it, the redeeming function of divine grace:

> ...his voice was propertied
> As all the tuned spheres,...
> For his bounty,
> There was no winter in't; an autumn 'twas
> That grew the more by reaping:...
> Think you there was, or might be, such a man
> As this I dream'd of?
> *Dolabella*:   Gentle madam, no.
> *Cleopatra*: You lie, up to the hearing of the gods.
> But, if there be, or ever were, one such,
> It's past the size of dreaming: v, ii, 83–97

We have here transcended the material world, for in it no harvest can 'grow the more by reaping'. Another Shakespearean heroine knew the same truth:

> My bounty is as boundless as the sea,
> My love as deep; the more I give to thee,
> The more I have, for both are infinite.
>
> *Romeo and Juliet*, ii, ii, 133–5

---

[1] Cf. *Merchant of Venice*, iii, ii, where such a feeling is explicitly contrasted with the love which gives and hazards all it has.

[2] Sonnet 129.

It is only love of all the gifts possible between human beings of which it can be said that it grows by being given away and lives by sacrificing itself. In this it is, however, akin to the 'grace' which men may hope to receive from a divine source untrammelled by the limitations of time and space. It is like grace also in that it is entirely unrelated to desert, and although the heart may be deliberately opened to receive it, it can never be won by force or demanded as a right. Without it men and women wander, lost souls in outer darkness.

Antony and Cleopatra offers no false consolations, no hope of evading the inevitable consequences of defying the established and accepted social order—such consequences may be transcended, but they are not removable in the actual world. In *The Tempest* it is significant that Shakespeare returns in one respect to the pattern of *Measure for Measure*, for all the elaborate evil intended is never actually carried out. Isabella forgives Angelo when she believes he has murdered Claudio, but when Angelo is spared death and given a fresh chance of happiness in this world, his victim in actual fact has not died.

His act did not o'ertake his bad intent.   v, i, 452

Shakespeare's drama tells of man's life as it is lived within this world's limits of time and space, and in those terms a 'happy ending' is shown as dependent on extreme evil having been avoided. When King Hamlet, Desdemona or Duncan has been killed, then the story is inevitably tragic. Even in *The Tempest*, the play which has most to say about the possibility of repentance and the beauty of mercy, there is nothing which suggests that there is any way of avoiding the fundamental truth that what is actually sown somebody will inevitably reap. Yet man must pardon the sower of the intolerable harvest, for though Shakespeare never pretends that human repentance and human pardon can avert the consequences of wrongdoing, the plays consistently illuminate the beauty and importance of both, so that we are encouraged to believe that they are in accord with some essential quality of life.

Antony and Cleopatra and *The Tempest* are a long step from *The*

Parliament of Heaven in which the Four Daughters of God kissed each other on the stage at 'N—Town' or from the Doomsday plays in which, all false-seeming stripped away at last, the risen souls are divided into the saved and the damned. We are offered no final solution; the old patterns are cracked and strained; the great drive to imaginative exploration into reality, whether it was deliberate or largely unconscious, has broken through the closed system of Elizabethan–Christian thought to which Shakespeare's mind had for so long submitted. We are here in no sheltering tabernacle at the end of the journey, yet neither are we lost in the wilderness. From the riches of the medieval world much had to be jettisoned of both security and peace of mind, but much was retained. Throughout his creative work Shakespeare remains concerned with those elements of man's experience which are central to Christianity, and the values which he attributes to them remain the Christian values, but at the end his thought could not be confined by a theological system nor his poetic imagination by theological symbolism. The last plays dealing, as did the first, with the transcendental values of good, evil, justice and mercy yet differ from their predecessors by placing these concepts firmly within the limits of time and space. Men must bring each other mercy and must replace the pursuit of justice by that of love. Thus, if at all, the music of the spheres may at last be made audible, sounded by men for man.

> For Mercy, Pity, Peace, and Love
> Is God, our Father dear,
> And Mercy, Pity, Peace, and Love
> Is Man, his child and care.
>
> For Mercy has a human heart,
> Pity a human face,
> And Love, the human form divine,
> And Peace, the human dress.
>
> Then every man, of every clime,
> That prays in his distress,
> Prays to the human form divine,
> Love, Mercy, Pity, Peace.[1]

[1] *Writings of William Blake*, Nonesuch Press, 1957, *Songs of Innocence*, The Divine Image.

INDEX

QUOTATIONS AND REFERENCES